GROUP AS A WHOLE

GROUP AS A WHOLE
Learning for Leadership, Authority and Organisation

Lionel F. Stapley

KARNAC
firing the mind

First published in 2024 by
Karnac Books Limited
62 Bucknell Road
Bicester
Oxfordshire OX26 2DS

British Library Cataloguing in Publication Data

A C.I.P. for this book is available from the British Library

ISBN: 978-1-80013-123-1 (paperback)
ISBN: 978-1-80013-122-4 (e-book)
ISBN: 978-1-80013-121-7 (PDF)

Typeset by Medlar Publishing Solutions Pvt Ltd, India

www.firingthemind.com

Contents

About the author

Lionel F. Stapley is an internationally recognised author, fellow of OPUS, organisational consultant, and psychodynamic and executive coach working with individuals, groups, and organisations in both the public and private sectors across the UK and Europe, as well as South America, China, Hong Kong, Russia, Slovenia, Poland, and Ghana.

He is also a commercially focused consultant, engaging with major public and private sector organisations at a senior level to help deliver their strategic objectives. He has a proven record of growing brand recognition and of successfully managing and developing the reputation of an international educational charity that seeks to encourage the reflective citizen.

Lionel is also a chartered fellow of both the CIPD and the CIM and a member of the International Society for the Psychoanalytic Study of Organizations (ISPSO).

Author's note

For ease of reading, when non-specific situations are being referred to, "he" is used throughout but the points raised are applicable to all.

Introduction

The context for group relations learning

The first group relations conference in the United Kingdom was held in 1957, co-organised by the University of Leicester and the Tavistock Institute of Human Relations (TIHR). This event was inspired by work at the National Training Laboratory (NTL) in the USA, and was based on T Groups, a model of intensive experiential learning that had evolved from the work of the social psychologist, Kurt Lewin.

Most of those involved in setting up TIHR in 1947 were social scientists and psychodynamically oriented psychiatrists who had been using group approaches to tackle wartime's problems. Among those working together during the war, a number had pre-war links with the Tavistock Clinic. This had been set up after the First World War as an outpatient psychiatric clinic, with a psychoanalytic orientation, and had become an important centre for training psychiatrists and allied professionals. When the National Health Service was set up the Tavistock Clinic became part of it. At this point, a new home had to be found for its non-clinical activities, especially the social department, and TIHR was founded for this purpose.

Lewin's insistence on the importance of studying the gestalt properties of groups as a whole is the basis for understanding the purpose of group relations learning.

Vital to the further understanding of GR is the contribution of the psychoanalyst Wilfred Bion who was similarly focusing on the group as a whole. He postulated that at any given time the behaviour of a group can be analysed at two levels: as a sophisticated group (or work group) met to perform an overt task; and at the same time as a basic group, acting on one, and only one, of three covert basic assumptions (fight–flight; dependency; and pairing) to which its individual members contribute anonymously and in ways of which they are not consciously aware.

Bion's formulation was one of the psychoanalytic components of the GR framework. A second is the formulation by Melanie Klein of processes of infant development and their effects on adult life (e.g. Klein, 1959). She identified the "paranoid–schizoid" position as that early phase of development in which the infant does not distinguish between inside and outside. The dominant anxiety in that stage is paranoid and the dominant defence to cope with that anxiety is schizoid—an unconscious splitting of the "good object" (the gratifying breast, mother) from the "bad object" (the deprived breast, also mother). These primitive processes of splitting and projection are never wholly overcome, and they are constantly reactivated in adult life in relations, for example between followers and leaders, between groups, and between nations. They are the stuff of basic assumption behaviour which Bion linked to psychotic anxiety and mechanisms of splitting and projective identification, characteristics of the paranoid–schizoid and depressive positions (Bion, 1961, p. 164).

Psychoanalysis, besides suggesting that explanations for human behaviour in groups may be found in primitive and unconscious processes, also provided a role model for the Tavistock working with groups and organisations. This is a form of action research in which the researcher is also a consultant, taking a professional role in relation to the client system; and consultancy is the method through which research data is generated. Individuals and groups interact in order to find ways of giving meaning to their experience and also to develop mechanisms that can defend them against uncertainty and anxiety. These defences, often unrecognisable and deeply rooted, are threatened by prospects of change, hence it is an important part of the consultant's role to serve as a container during the "working through" of change.

A further, more specific derivation from the analyst's role is the stress laid on examining and using the transference and countertransference within the professional relationship. That is to say, the feelings evoked in him may offer evidence of underlying and unstated issues and feelings in the client system: that which is repressed by the client may be expressed by the consultant. Again, this was a cornerstone of Bion's approach to groups.

From this basic understanding, group relations learning developed across the world. In 1965 A. K. (Ken) Rice published a volume titled *Learning for Leadership*, a brilliant description of group relations as it was at that time—a volume which is still an important and recommended reading for those interested in group relations.

Since that time, over the years, group relations has developed considerably, Perhaps the most important description of new developments was that of Eric Miller, who was the Tavistock director of the group relations training programme, in his Tavistock Occasional Paper "The 'Leicester' model" (1989).

An overview and deeper understanding of group relations learning

The normal way the group relations conference starts is when the CEO or chair of an organisation or institute commissions a director to direct the conference.

The director then selects the staff and invites them to take up roles in the conference, at the same time requesting them to authorise him as the director. When the invited staff respond, they authorise the director and the director authorises them to take up their roles in the conference. Thus, all members of staff are duly authorised from the beginning.

There will then follow a staff meeting chaired by the director, who will emphasise that while they are informed that everything they do will be done for the benefit of the learning of the members, they will also be in a learning role. This is important as staff may have experience of previous conferences, but it is the experience of this unique conference that staff will need to work with: to study the behaviour of this group, as a group, as it happens.

The meeting will consist of all staff, including the administrator, and any training consultants. The latter will be delegated to hold review meetings with an experienced staff member. The staff meeting will provide the opportunity to share deployment of staff, details of the membership, the membership of the small study groups, and the review and application groups.

It will also provide an opportunity to prepare for the opening of the conference, the seating arrangements, introductions, and essential information for the members. If possible, the meeting will end with a walkthrough of the territory, to familiarise staff with the working rooms.

Continuous professional development (CPD)

If we are to develop a high-quality group relations learning programme, it will be appreciated that continuous staff development is important.

In-conference development

Group relations events are learning events for all staff as well as members. All consultants work with more senior consultants in one-to-one CPD meetings, where they can further their understanding of the group relations learning and the consultant role.

Annual CPD workshop

The purpose of this event is to ensure that group relations staff are continuing the aim of providing high-quality group relations learning for all staff. This event is open to all group relations consulting staff, no matter what their experience is. This annual CPD event is facilitated by a director and highly qualified colleague who will identify and provide opportunities for understanding various vital aspects of taking up a consultant role.

Ongoing development of new staff

To meet growing needs, it will be necessary to continually seek to develop new staff.

This volume describes the current theory and practice of group relations conferences as followed by IGO consultants in various countries.

IGO Consultancy Services Ltd works with groups and organisations worldwide, the author of this volume is the director of the organisation. IGO provides consultancy for culture change, mergers, and other organisational needs. A further important role is psychodynamic and executive coaching for individuals, and group relations conferences in China (Beijing, Hong Kong, and Shanghai), Russia, and Poland, as well as the UK.

In regards to group relations conferences, it has always been the aim of IGO to provide high-quality learning by competent consulting and managing staff. This is achieved by a process whereby prospective consultants attend at least two substantive group relations conferences as members, followed by membership of the IGO dedicated, residential 'Advanced Training in Small Group Processes Workshop' which is by invitation only for a maximum of six people.

This provides members with a sound knowledge of group relations dynamics which is then added to by taking a training consultant role working with an experienced small group consultant, who also provides continuing professional development (CPD). If all goes well, individuals can become competent small group consultants.

The anticipated outcomes of this book are to enable readers to understand the way that "beneath the surface", mainly emotional and unconscious dynamics affect us all in regard to our meaning-making and decision-making involving other people, other groups, and changed circumstances; and to enable readers to apply this learning directly to their group relations learning experiences.

The focus of this volume is on groups. Here the intention is to go beyond taking things at their face value by going deeper and exploring the underlying, less evident phenomena concerning groups that occur beneath the surface. The more frequently used approach is to study the behaviour of the individuals in a group. This is one way of creating an understanding of group behaviour. However, the approach taken here is to study groups from the perspective of the group as a whole. In doing so, we can identify that which will provide a totally different perspective. Thus, while a focus on individual actions and relationships in groups is a valid field of study, there is this other level, the *group as a whole*, which becomes the unit of study from a more encompassing perspective.

This volume is based on a series of six seminars that the author arranged with colleagues who are members of group relations China, as a means of providing a deeper understanding of *group as a whole* learning. It was understood that Covid-19 would prevent any opportunity to hold group relations conferences in China for some while. These seminars, based on the IGO Model of group relations, were intended to involve Chinese consultants in the "normal Continuing Professional Development Programme" that was an annual event.

The chapters

The chapters take the reader through pre-conference activity, particularly the need for "authority", and a discussion on the importance and understanding of the group as a whole.

The six chapters, which follow the usual structure of IGO group relations conferences, are now arranged as follows:

Chapter 1	The field of study—the group as a whole
Chapter 2	Consultancy skills and knowledge
Chapter 3	The small study group (SSG)
Chapter 4	The large study group (LSG)
Chapter 5	The inter-group (IG) event—(day 3)
Chapter 6	Review and application groups (RAG)

The aim of these chapters is to develop a deeper understanding of group relations learning. It is in no way a substitute for the vital learning from experiential opportunities provided by group relations conferences, whereby we are able to learn from the way that we take up roles or are mobilised by the group to take up roles, and to understand that our valency can result in us being used repeatedly in the same way. This learning is rich and valuable because it happens in the here and now, and is our direct experience.

These chapters will largely concentrate on the theories that are being used and applied in group relations conferences. There is a whole field of theoretical learning, some of it complex in nature, some not always easily understood when we are being controlled by our emotions, and some unconscious processes that we are not familiar with. There will be an element of repetition of the theory throughout the chapters to enable understanding.

It will be helpful for the reader to explore their own experiences in being a member of, or working as a consultant in, group relations conferences. From this process, readers will get in touch with actual emotions that are experienced at the time. In this manner, the learning opportunities will provide powerful insights to individuals and other group members.

CHAPTER 1

The field of study—the group as a whole

An introduction to the group as a whole

We may speak for convenience about the individual and the group, but in practice, these two can never be separated and should not be considered even theoretically in isolation. Physical assembly of people into a group simply makes "political" characteristics of human beings more easily demonstrable. None of us, however "isolated in time and space, should be regarded as outside a group or lacking in active manifestations of group psychology" (Bion, 1961, p. 168). We carry our "groupishness" with us all the time. It is clear that everything is embedded in the social context of our lives, particularly in the dominant primary group, the family, and it is really a social psychology. As will be shown, the behaviour observed in groups is not to be considered a product of groups as such but of the fact that the "human being is a group animal".

The group as a whole is a level of analysis that represents processes that may be more or less than the sum of the individual members of the group and their interpersonal dynamics. The group as a whole can be conceptualised as behaving in a different manner from, but related to, the dynamics of the members. Indeed, many of the defences or means of coping with anxiety used in groups are variations of individual behaviour. From this vantage point, groups as a whole have their own dynamics resulting from the interactions of group members who are interdependent members and subsystems. In effect, the group becomes a thing; it is reified as if a group mind exists, and it is experienced as being as real as an individual's brain in which thinking and feeling occur.

Throughout this chapter I will expose and explore the way that mainly unconscious dynamics beneath the surface of groups are as important as those concerning individuals.

Some of the beneath-the-surface dynamics that occur in groups and organisations are similar to those described in the ways that we as individuals develop defences as a means of avoiding and defending against anxiety, and are also replicated, albeit in a slightly different manner, in groups and organisations. As you will discover, this is not surprising as groups evoke feelings associated with the maternal holding environment. So that, when members of groups experience frustration and anxiety, they are likely to respond by using primitive processes such as splitting, projection, and introjection. At a group level, these defences result in important phenomena that will be described and referred to as social structures used as a defence against anxiety.

We will probably all be familiar with the notion that the performance of a team is superior to the individual efforts of the members: that the sum is greater than the parts. This is a helpful starting position in beginning to understand something of the dynamics concerned. What though, we might ask, is this team or group? We will also be familiar with frequent references to the notion of a group mind or of groups behaving as an organism. Indeed, it is not uncommon for some to erroneously speak of organisations as actively doing something or other. Again, we may ask, how can this be? We know that only individuals have minds and that no such thing as a group mind exists. It is individual human beings who are constantly engaged in the process of meaning-making. Or, to put it another way, it is not about the doing which a human does, it is about the doing which a human is. How or why, then, do we develop the idea that a "group mind" exists?

What we can say is that groups act "as if" they have a group mind. But you may well say that this still begs the question, how does this come about? Clearly, individuals must be involved in making sense of their surrounding experience, and it must, therefore, be individuals who are concerned with the development of this phenomenon which resembles a group mind. We may reflect that there is no feeling, no experience, no thought, no perception independent of a meaning-making context in which it becomes a feeling, an experience, a thought, a perception, because we are the meaning-making context. If the members of a group as human beings did not take in their various sensations and translate them into something, they would not be what they are. It would seem then that the group is a construct and that without individual human activity, the construct of the group as a whole simply would not exist.

Influence of the maternal holding environment

In seeking an explanation that will enable us to understand how the vitally important construct of a group as a whole comes about we need to return to the earliest days of human existence. The reader may need little reminding that when born, the infant is totally dependent on his mother for both psychological and social support. The mother provides what might helpfully be referred to as a maternal holding environment. Holding in the mother's womb and then holding in the mother's arms is the first boundary out of chaos within which the infant's personality can develop. The early relation in the maternal holding environment is characterised by infantile dependence, that is, a dependence based on a primary identification with the object, and an inability to differentiate and adapt.

The need for attachment to the mother is such that individuals are so completely dependent on others during infancy that they cannot survive without eliciting responses from their parents or other carers. The infant's journey from dependency to separation is somewhat of a struggle, and it would appear that the infant is involved in a series of repeated separations and reunions with the mother. Each step of psychological independence is welcomed for the sense of freedom but feared for the threat of abandonment, isolation, and loss of object love. We are never totally independent even after "me" and "not me" have been established. Perhaps, then, it is not surprising that this experience stays with us and is so influential throughout our lives. Deep in our unconscious is a strong and impenetrable bond with our mother that lasts forever, and there is always a danger of regressing to the comfortable dependent position. Such was that bond that none of us dares to give up our inborn need for maternal gratification. None of us is truly independent, even in adult life, and from time to time we cling to each other as if we are mothers to each other.

The individual is part of a group from earliest infancy, initially a group of two, the mother–infant dyad, then a group of three or more as the existence of father and siblings has to be accommodated and later a series of overlapping family and social groups. These coexist in external reality and in the developing of the individual's internal world. A result is that which I shall refer to as "groupishness" and the need and yearning for the "good" mother which are believed to reside in the very core of our being. These are connected to the need for a favourable emotional response from the mother that has been described as being necessary for the well-being or very existence of the infant. It is thus that the group entity can become for the individual the symbolic representation of a nurturing mother.

Being a member of a group will trigger unconscious feelings associated with our early and highly potent emotional maternal bond so that we are not only reminded of that situation but treat the group as if it were the maternal holding environment. Terms such as "mother earth" and "motherland" or even "alma mater" which are used popularly, are of relevance here. In a broader sense, the hypothesis can be advanced that our human needs to belong and to establish a state of psychological unity with others, represent a covert wish for restoring an earlier state of unconflicted well-being inherent in the exclusive union with mother. Put another way, we seek to recreate in the present-day group a holding environment that will provide us with the same sort of psychological and social support that we experienced in the maternal holding environment.

A result of our individual ability to form concepts means that we can construct an object in the mind that is a non-human object. The group is to be seen as such an artificial creation; it is a mental construct. More than this though, it is a mental construct that develops out of our internalised pool of knowledge and feelings of the maternal holding environment. Thus, the construct that is "group" becomes the nurturing mother that we unconsciously feel will provide the psychological and social support previously experienced. We need the group to provide us with a favourable emotional response as much as we needed mother to do so. A measure of the importance that the group has for us is perhaps illustrated by the way we quickly come to identify with a group.

Any of us who have experienced the process of joining a group, even in a temporary situation, will reflect how this became "our" group and that this group took on a form of identity for us. Our group also had boundaries which determined who was a member of that group and who was not. Having created the construct of a group or organisation, it is reified and the members of the group act "as if" it exists and, because of our experience, even if the object is not human, it is associated with human activity. A result is that we, therefore, attach to this object the same attributes as other influential objects, especially the mother. We attach to the group (held in the mind) the same emotions so that, to a lesser or greater degree, the members of a group will experience the same feelings. We sometimes get an indication of this when members of an organisation speak of the organisation as "not caring" or of it being a "really caring" organisation.

Groupishness

At its core, the group-as-a-whole perspective is derived from the construct of "group in the mind", which is held to be similar to that of "mother in the mind". As previously discussed, out of the totality of our early experience through the process of introjection, the infant creates a construct that is "mother in the mind". "My Mum" is the view of mother as seen by the infant. This view of mother in the mind affects the way the infant behaves because he wishes to please mother and not to make her angry, as, at this stage, she is the source of all pleasure. Individual behaviour in groups is seen to equate with the unconscious reactions and manoeuvres of infants in relation to the ambivalently held mothering object. Consequently, we might well anticipate that the group in the mind will also affect the way group members behave because they will view the group as the source of all pleasure. We may also expect that when members of groups experience frustration and anxiety, they are likely to respond by using primitive processes such as splitting, projection, and introjection.

Since all individuals go through the experiences of infancy, we can be sure that the most outstanding and most continuous of human psychic needs is that of emotional responses from other individuals. We will recall that the individual is so completely dependent at this stage that he cannot survive without eliciting emotional responses from mother. Attachment is a deep and universal need, and we all know what it means to be alone in a crowd. In adult life, it is this need for a response, and especially for a favourable response, which provides individuals with their main stimulus to socially acceptable behaviour. People abide by the mores of their groups and societies quite as much because they desire approval as because they fear punishment. The way that members of a group unconsciously treat the group as the maternal holding environment is because the need for attachment is so strong. This will, in turn, have the effect of achieving greater and closer groupishness by which process a number of individuals unconsciously develop the concept of being one, of being a group.

But this may not provide a full explanation. The individual's very belief that a group exists as a separate entity can be seen as regression. Regression to a state where, to put it crudely, the group is mother, but before mother was experienced as a person entirely distinct from other significant members of the family constellation and before that "other" was clearly established. As with the infant relating to the mother, the adult must establish contact with the emotional life of the group in which he lives or works. This task would appear to be as formidable to the adult as the relationship with the breast appears to be to the infant, and the failure to meet the demands of this task is revealed in his regression. The creation of the concept of the "group in the mind" and the subsequent belief that a group exists, as distinct from an aggregate of individuals, is an essential part of the regression.

The group-as-mother analogy fundamentally draws the parallels between infant in relation to mother and individual in relation to group. The central thrust here is that the group situation creates such ambivalence and anxiety that it unconsciously returns the group members to earlier relationships with mother and evokes all of the psychosocial mechanisms involved.

In sum, groups in a similar manner to the mothering object create strong, conflicting, ambivalent feelings of love and hate, bliss and despair, dread and joy. Primitive ambivalence, anxiety, and regression are generated as a consequence of the fact that the group represents the primal mother. The natural psychological habitat of man is the group, but man's adaptation to that habitat is imperfect, a state of affairs which is reflected in his chronic ambivalence towards groups. Group membership is psychologically essential and yet a source of increasing discomfort.

A further explanation may lie in the notion of identification. Identification brings into play such functions as adaptation to reality, reality testing, a sense of reality, the self concept (with its self and object relations), and the capacity to form object relationships. Questions such as, "Who am I?", "Where have I been?", "Where am I going?" are deeply ensconced in the individual's group experiences from within the family and outside it. Since most human needs are supplied by other persons, adaptation to the world is to the world of other people and not to the world of nature. This provides a further impetus for our groupishness. Members of a group test reality by comparing their own perceptions and evaluations with those of other group members who experience the same or similar events. The "truth" of reality concepts is developed in the bubbling cauldron of consensus, not in the isolation of lonely contemplation. Members of groups test reality by comparing their perceptions and evaluations with those of other persons who experience the same or similar experiences. This may result in shared qualities, interests, or ideals being capable of precipitating identifications with others or identification as an emotional tie between people. In this way, reality testing—the need for consistency, continuity, and confirmation—may lead to consensual validation.

Identification with a group in the mind goes beyond the mere perception of it and the investing of it with some emotional element, for identification in this sense also contains an element of responding, or, more specifically, an element of individual commitment. The result of an individual's group identification is that he reacts to the attributes of the group as if these attributes were also his. A striking illustration is the way an individual reacts to a criticism or slight of his group as if he himself had been criticised or slighted. To belong to or to feel part of a group also implies a more or less transient giving up of some aspect of the individual's self to the group as a group.

The individual and the group

As for identification with the group as a whole, the process can per-haps be best explored within the framework of the individual group member's perception. At any moment of his group membership, each individual can be said to perceive selected aspects of an existing social situation. That may include interacting group members and a central person or central persons, but also the group as a whole. As a result of identification with the group as a whole, the group is no longer viewed through its individual components; rather, the group holding environment is seen "as if" it were an organism—an entity in its own right, possessing dynamics, structures, and development independent of and reaching beyond the individuals who make it up. To the extent that the focus is on the individual, he is to be viewed as a representative of the group for which he stands, and in turn the manner in which he is treated represents relatedness to this entire group.

Of central theoretical and practical interest to groups is what I term "relatedness": the process of mutual influence between individual and group, group and group, and group and organisation. And, we might go beyond this to consider the relatedness of organisation to commu-nity and to wider social systems, to society itself. In all these forms of relatedness there is a potential tension. The individual needs groups in order to establish their identity, to find meaning in their existence, and to express different aspects of themselves. Correspondingly the group also needs the individual member for its own collective purposes—both to contribute to the group's task and also to participate in the processes through which the group acquires and maintains its own distinctive identity. This provides a further impetus for our groupishness, but this process is one that often threatens individuality.

The group being viewed as a whole, as an organism or an entity in its own right that possesses dynamics, structure, and development inde-pendent of the individual, has the effect of reducing the individual to being part of the whole. The individual is but a component element of the group who may be viewed as being representative of the group and acting on behalf of the group. Freud took notice of individual behaviour only so far as it was expressive of developments in the group as a whole. That is to say, if a group member attacked the leader, he would attempt to interpret why this was being done on behalf of the group at a given moment—neglecting, although he was fully aware of the fact, that this behaviour was also meaningful to the individual in the light of his own particular history. To put it another way, we take the object of analysis to be all the evidence produced by group members that we believe belongs to a group: the common fantasies, the concerted behaviours, and tacit agreements that point to the existence of a shared group mentality. Thus we are concerned with the way that an individual is mobilised by the group to do something on its behalf; there is an assumption that individuals are speaking on behalf of the group and not as individuals; they are representing the group.

Our primary focus in groups needs to be the group as a whole, and this includes what individuals or subgroups may do. Roles that are taken up by group members are a function of the group as a whole and the behaviour of a person in a group has more to do with the group than it does with his individuality. I should stress that I am not here referring to formal, allocated roles. What I am referring to are roles that members of a group unconsciously take on as a result of beneath-the-surface processes. In other words, any role taken by an individual member of a group may be considered to be a group role, one that is a function of group dynamics. When role is defined as a property of the group, then role prescriptions are filled, sometimes by individuals, sometimes by subgroups, and sometimes by identifiable clusters of behaviour that are a group property and serve a role function, although they appear independent from all individual members or subgroups. These group role dynamics are to be seen as a manifestation of the group as a whole.

As we have seen, group processes are indeed different from individual dynamics, and specific group dynamics occur that are of a different nature than individual dynamics, albeit that they have their origins in the individual. All of the beneath-the-surface activity referred to will have an effect on every single group because that's what a group is; and that's what a group does. To summarise, the group as a whole phenomenon assumes that individuals and subgroups are vehicles that reflect and express the group as a whole. Individual group members are acting together unconsciously as a collusive whole in which their interactions and shared fantasies create and represent at once the group as a whole. It is from this premise that an individual speaking or acting in a group is perceived as expressing aspects of the group. This is so, whether we are referring to a family group, a residents' group, a small group with responsibility for a particular task in an organisation, a whole department, or an entire organisation. Each group will be unique and its continuing experiences will be unique. The unique features of each group will be part of the consideration as to how it is experienced.

Consultancy skills and knowledge

Note: Chapter 2 provides a basis for all subsequent chapters and, as such, may well be required reading to explain and understand what follows.

In this chapter, I shall describe a typical conference, bearing in mind that different versions may contain different elements. However, they share a common task: to provide the individual with opportunities for learning about the way in which he functions in the setting provided by the conference and its various groupings. This "learning from experience", learning in vivo, may then be extrapolated to the world outside the closed system of the conference.

I shall describe the theoretical base, followed by the structure, and follow this with a discussion of the consultant's role, which will bring in elements of both.

Theory

The theoretical base for this approach to learning derives from two main sources that were brought together in the development of group relations learning by the Tavistock Institute of Human Relations: they are, psychoanalysis and open systems theory.

The input from psychoanalysis

In terms of psychoanalysis, it is from Wilfred Bion, and particularly from Bion's own method of learning about groups (described in *Experiences in Groups*), that the group relations approach has evolved. Here, I want to emphasise how brief is Bion's description of a group at work (the work group), compared to his analyses of a group when functioning in more primitive and unconscious "anti-work" modes (the basic assumptions, discussed in detail on pp. 15–21).

Bion gives us three ideas that are essential to the business of group relations:

- The concept of valency
- The notion of a group unconscious
- The notion of the move back and forth between work group and basic assumption functioning.

Valency

The concept of valency has, since Bion's time, been given much attention in the context of group relations. In terms of the learning and deductions from group relations and from organisational consultancy, it is clear that the individual's valencies are larger than a simple predetermination towards a particular basic assumption. Our various individual psychic vulnerabilities also serve as valencies, so that the group will appear to choose the same individual again and again to express something that will seem to be as much about that individual as it is about the group's functioning. Thus, teams will often come to ask for consultancy on the grounds that there are "personality clashes".

The group unconscious

One way of looking at the propensity for individuals repeatedly to take up particular positions is to imagine that we could view the unconscious in the way that infra-red binoculars allow us to view things at night: we would then see flashing neon signs on every one of us with statements like, "oedipal issues this way," and "You want paranoia, here I am." It is worth noting that there may also exist a group valency as well as that which belongs to the individuals.

Bion's view of the "group unconscious" was that of a universal unconscious embracing and underlying the functioning of the entire species. His use of the term relates to what takes place when a particular group is formed for a particular reason. He believed that when this happens, individuals enter into an unconscious collusion that resembles a primitive form of organisation, the "group mentality", that recruits members to itself. The group unconscious emerges in the face of the fundamental anxieties that assault every individual faced with the prospect of becoming part of a group.

The mechanism responsible for this process of "becoming a member of a group" is the individual's valency, or propensity for adopting or falling into one or another of the basic assumption modes of functioning.

For example:

- One individual may incline towards a dependent state of mind (basic assumption dependency) within a group
- Another may take up a belligerent stance, another an anxious, timid position (basic assumption fight–flight), and
- Yet another, seek for a partner or soulmate to cling to (basic assumption pairing).

Bion's view was that such valencies are part of the biological or physiological aspect of our psyche, part of human heritage. It was their very existence, he thought, that enabled the individual to become part of a group.

However, it is this same capacity that raises anxiety, because the individual becomes alarmed at the prospect of becoming merged with or submerged in the group mind—and thereby his own mind, or individuality. Bion felt that the idea of a primitive group unconscious that, developmentally speaking, precedes the individual's unconscious, is in fact a kind of theory developed by groups themselves to account for the anxiety they are experiencing.

In other words, it is a symptom of the group experience, rather than being a rational construct. This is, of course, a metaphor, but the notion of a "group mind" can be helpful when it comes to understanding some of the phenomena that take place in groups. Indeed, the group relations tradition makes much use of this concept in understanding organisations, and consultants often see their aim, during the diagnostic phase of the consultation, as identifying and describing what they call the "organisational mind".

The work group

A simple description of the work group is that it is a real or conscious process, where the group is working to task in a collaborative way. The following provides greater clarity. Central to the health of a group, Bion thought there was a broader question: What is a group? His central tenet was that in every group the group behaves as if there were actually two groups present. He thought of this as a prevailing unconscious phantasy. He observed that the two groups present were comprised of a "work group" and a "basic assumption group". The work group seems aware of its purpose and concerns itself with its "real"—that is to say, its consciously acknowledged—task. The members of the work group cooperate as separate individuals and can recognise skills and qualities in themselves as well as in their leader. They allow themselves to be led in so far as this is useful to the task of the group. However, Bion also saw that it was actually most unusual for groups to behave in this sensible fashion. Instead, they seem to develop attitudes and methods that are not in the service of the tasks that have been agreed. He observed that a group appears to make certain basic assumptions about itself, and it is these assumptions that mostly determine how the group operates and whether it is able to function as a work group at all.

Bion writes:

> Work-group activity is obstructed, diverted, and on occasion assisted, by certain other mental activities that have in common the attribute of powerful emotional drives. These activities, at first sight chaotic are given a certain cohesion if it is assumed that they spring from basic assumptions common to all the group. (1961, p. 145)

Basic assumptions

In effect, members of the group create a "basic assumption" by contributing selectively unconscious elements. This anonymous collaboration creates a group mentality which expresses the unanimous but unspoken aims and beliefs of the group. But this group mentality destroys any possibility of any individual privacy. An individual seeking to join the emotional life of a group makes efforts as formidable as an infant seeking the mother's breast. If these efforts are frustrated, they regress and such regression is to the state referred to above where the individual is under the impression that he is omnipotent and that they are in possession of a magical capacity that can realise all their wishes by simply imagining the satisfaction of them.

At a social level the members of the group continue to act as if they were adults and the unknowing observer would barely detect any change in their behaviour. However, when they are functioning in a basic assumption mode they are acting at a deeply unconscious level as if they were in the maternal holding environment when omnipotence and magical thinking brought them all they needed to satisfy their feelings. All basic assumption functioning has this same quality but there are variations in the functioning of these groups which can be deduced from observation of such a group. The particular behaviour of the group provides us with the clues as to the type of basic assumption that the group is met to pursue. And this will in turn provide the information that it is not operating as a work group. I should stress that this is a totally unconscious and collusive process that is operating at the level of a group as a whole.

Three specific types of basic assumption were originally identified and although others have been identified since, these three remain the most significant. Each of these three types of behaviour can be seen to connect to our earliest experiences. These types of functioning can be observed in all sorts of groups and in all manner of circumstances. They can be said to coexist with the functioning of the work group and the group may move from one to the other form of functioning. The three types of basic assumptions are: basic assumption dependence; basic assumption fight–flight; and basic assumption pairing, and these are explained separately below.

Basic assumption dependency

In a group where the basic assumption is of dependence, the group seeks the support of a leader from whom it hopes to receive spiritual and material guidance, protection, and nurture. It believes that all its needs can be satisfied by one person, on whom it develops total dependence. Bion asks us to take this in a literal, not a metaphorical, sense. At first, members of the group try to reinforce the idea that the group comprises a consultant and his or her members. They insist that the consultant is the leader, and the only important person there. They feel cared for only when they are directly relating to the consultant. If they are not relating, they feel frustrated and trapped in their need and hunger. For this type of group, power is something that is magical rather than scientific: the ideal leader is something of a sorcerer.

There is a regression into the state of merging of the early mother–child dyad; the group wishes to attain security through one person. The members of the group mentally act as if they are totally without constructive thought or ideas: and, despite the fact that they are now adults, as if they were inadequate and immature children. The group treats the leader as some sort of godlike individual who is perceived as omnipotent and omniscient: an all-knowing and all-doing leader who has the capability of achieving anything and everything. Very often, the member mobilised also accepts this position in the group and is drawn into enacting his part in this basic assumption, making all the decisions for the group and generally doing all the thinking. The group may persist in this state for some while, often forming the belief that if they only wait long enough the leader will produce the sought-for magic cure. Eventually the leader will be experienced as not meeting the group's expectations of achieving this totally impossible task. At this stage, other leaders may be encouraged to take on the role but they will all suffer the same fate as the original leader.

One can see immediately why it might be common for groups struggling to understand the task to fall into a basic assumption of dependency and to find a member who, they insist, is all-powerful, wise, and loving. Though the group strives to defend itself against inevitable disappointment by holding tenaciously to its conviction, invariably the leader disappoints and the group turns to mobilise a new leader, destined to suffer the same fate.

Basic assumption pairing

The second type of basic assumption concerns the group's aims in uniting. Bion was drawn to recognition of this problem by a recurring situation: the discussion would become monopolised by two people who would seem more or less to ignore the presence of other members of the group. The gender of the individuals is of little significance. From time to time the couple would exchange glances in such a way as to suggest an amorous relationship. In the meantime, their conversation was not very different, in its content, from other conversational exchanges in the group. While neurotics are usually very impatient with any activity that does not refer to their own problems, members of the group may accept this monopolisation of the conversation by the couple with apparent ease.

In the pairing state, two members of the group with a valency towards a notion that everything will be alright and that the world is a hopeful place may take up their role in a variety of ways. The group enjoys the optimism presented by the pair and listens to what is being said with great interest. The group is living in hope of something magical occurring; a new leader; a new thought, or something else that will bring about a new life—something that will solve all the existing problems and lead them all to some sort of Utopia. It is the feelings or imaginings of hope and optimism that are important to the group functioning in the basic assumption pairing. It would appear that the sole aim is to be cocooned in a never-ending state of hope and optimism, which may be similar to life as experienced in the womb.

In personal relationships, something similar is not uncommonly expressed verbally in the idea that marriage will end all a couple's problems. For the pairing group, the fond hope is that at some future time there will be a revolution or a solution that will bring an end to all their difficulties. Once again, the group avoids the task of working for itself and, instead, nurtures the couple in the hope that they will come together to create a solution. The crucial aspect is not the future event itself, but a vacuous feeling of unfocused hope that characterises the pairing group and alerts us to its existence. For the feelings of hope to be sustained, it is essential that the leaders should remain unborn. It is a person or idea that will save the group—in fact, from the feelings of hatred, destructiveness, and despair of its own or of another group—but in order to do this, obviously, the messianic hope must never be fulfilled.

Basic assumption fight–flight

In the third type of basic assumption, group members unite for preservation in order to fight against or escape from a threat. The group can opt for either activity with apparent indifference—hence the name fight–flight, which are two sides of the same coin. Group members accept a leader whose demands offer them opportunities for fighting or for evasion. In this type of situation a consultant will quickly realise that the group unites easily around any proposition that expresses violent rejection of all psychological difficulty, or offers means of avoiding difficulty by creating an external enemy.

Clearly, in nations at war with each other, a fight–flight leader will be selected. However, particularly in a group relations group, there is a tendency for the most paranoid member to be selected for this task, so as to ensure that if there is no obvious enemy, one can be found. Here we see the domination of the pleasure principle and of magical thinking that the leader can solve their problems by ignoring reality and adopting a process of fight or flight.

The fight leader may lead the group in an attack on the consultant, on another part of the conference, or on a figment of imagination, an enemy that only exists as a phantasy. The attack will not be based on reality, rather all activity will be designed to circumvent the task. The flight leader will lead the group into a flight from reality, and frequently in such situations issues will be trivialised and humour will replace any notion of serious discussion. Basic assumption activity is never oriented towards reality but involves phantasy which is then impulsively and uncritically acted out.

Use of basic assumptions

Each of the three basic assumption patterns is characterised by a distinct emotional state. We have seen that basic assumptions are distinct from one another. Yet they also share certain qualities: they are instinctive, and no training or preparation is required to engage in them.

They are oriented not towards reality, but towards internal phantasy, acting upon this impulsively and uncritically There is no need for cooperation between group members at this level of functioning: instead, individuals naturally possess valency.

Groups can and do alternate from one basic assumption group activity to another basic assumption group activity. Thus, a group may move from acting as a dependency group to acting as a fight group and back again. At some stage, they may move to or regain contact with reality and start acting as a work group. We might view basic assumption groups as an interference with the work task, just as naughty primitive impulses may interfere with the sensible work of a mature person. The work group is a bit like the serious parent who has a responsible attitude to life; while the basic assumption group is a bit like playful children who want immediate satisfaction of their desires. Individuals seem to fear being overwhelmed by the basic assumptions and develop the need to return to the work group. It may be a possibility that basic assumption groups not only develop as an escape from anxiety but also provide an opportunity for individuals to regain their contact with reality once the anxiety has subsided after being in the basic assumption mode.

The phenomena associated with basic assumptions are analogous to defences against psychotic anxiety. The more powerful the group's basic assumption, the less it makes rational use of verbal communication. When influenced by basic assumptions the group behaves as if it is unable to use symbols. Instead of developing language as a method of thought, the group uses an existing language as a mode of action. When we consider that the regression of members of the group is to a stage before the development of symbols, we should, perhaps, not be surprised that communication is not rational. Basic assumption behaviour is a frequent beneath-the-surface activity in groups and one which is discernible to anyone who is able to avoid being overwhelmed by the emotions and to stay in touch with reality.

What underlies the basic assumptions?

In the article "Group dynamics: a re-view", Bion (1952) tackles the question of why should groups operate along these lines? Why do the basic assumptions exist at all? He draws our attention to the emotional plane in a group and emphasises that as well as being a convenient means of ordering some of the complex occurrences in groups, the basic assumptions are the product of complex fusions of emotions and ideas. Also, while it is possible to discern oedipal configurations in the basic assumption material (suggestive of later developmental phases), Bion maintains that the strength and quality of the emotions, as well as the way in which the psychic and somatic expressions are interlocked, point to their derivation from the earliest levels of psychological development. He points out that the consultant—and also the work-group function with which the consultant is identified—is invested with feelings "that would be quite appropriate to the enigmatic, brooding, and questioning Sphinx (in the oedipal myth) from whom disaster emanates". Here, Bion seems to be noticing the way in which the group is gripped by an extreme sense of dread and anxiety when it finds itself at the receiving end of a questioning attitude from its Sphinx-like consultant. He thought this becomes more comprehensible when the group's experience is considered in the light of the developmental perspective outlined by Melanie Klein (see "Primitive mental activity" later in this chapter).

Bion writes:

> My impression is that the group approximates too closely, in the minds of the individuals composing it, to very primitive phantasies about the contents of the mother's body [Klein]. The attempt to make a rational investigation of the dynamics of the group is therefore perturbed by fears, and mechanisms for dealing with them, which are characteristic of the paranoid-schizoid position. The investigation cannot be carried out without the stimulation and activation of these levels. (Bion, 1961, p. 161)

Bion realised therefore that the basic assumptions could be resolved into something more fundamental. They are expressions of, or reactions against, a more primary state. This also clarified why it is that a group constantly shifts between basic assumptions, and why, at any one time, one assumption or another may be preferred. When the pressure of anxiety stemming from contact with a particular underlying primitive state becomes too great, it will precipitate a change in the defensive action required to deal with it. For example, psychotic anxiety might be aroused when the pairing group is active if some of its components are too close to particular primitive part-objects to escape identification with them. At this point a new defence must be found in another basic assumption state.

He writes:

> basic assumptions now emerge as formations secondary to an extremely early primal scene worked out on a level of part objects, and associated with psychotic anxiety and mechanisms of splitting and projective identification such as Melanie Klein has described as characteristic of the paranoid-schizoid and depressive positions. (1961, p. 163)

Bion saw it as being of the utmost importance to work out very thoroughly the primitive primal scene as it discloses itself in the group.

Open systems theory

The open systems tradition developed out of the thinking of von Bertalanffy (1950) who described a "Theory of open systems in physics and biology" in his classic paper of that name. He presented a model of "intake, conversion and output", which connected a particular system to a particular environment. This model was recognised by a number of social scientists as immediately applicable to human behaviour in institutional contexts. Out of this approach there developed the idea of the "primary task"—that which the organisation must carry out successfully if the enterprise is to survive, and this was followed by the contributions of Eric Miller and A. K. Rice (Miller, 1989; Miller & Rice, 1967; Rice, 1965). The combination of these approaches with psychoanalysis is the essence of the group relations approach.

The group relations tradition developed its "knowledge base" through experience within the group relations trainings as well as from organisational consultation, in particular, through an approach that has become described as "action research".

Elliott Jaques' (1955) observations of a factory, influenced by Kurt Lewin's field theory as well as by open systems theory, quickly developed into an early example of Lewin's idea of action research (1951). At first, Jaques had arranged simply to observe industrial relations within the Glacier Metal Company, but he was then encouraged to engage as a consultant. His observations led him to recognise that one of the main obstacles to communication was the fact that each side held fixed views about the attitude of the other. These entrenched views made it possible to get on with the everyday life of the factory, but they interfered with any possibility of communication, particularly anything that might lead to change. Change always raises anxiety. Jaques realised that these "attitudes and beliefs" acted as a focus for groups within the factory and that these groups could be described as systems: indeed, these systems often became formalised in a structure.

Social systems as a defence against anxiety

Recognising that these structures functioned in a way that allowed the participants to avoid anxiety, Jaques coined the expression "social systems as a defence against anxiety". Later Isabel Menzies Lyth (1960), using that same phrase as part of her title, described these defences clearly in a seminal paper about the training of nurses in a teaching hospital. She described a rigid structure that was experienced by the nurses as highly persecutory. The nurses experienced those above them in the hierarchy as keeping a close and suspicious watch upon them, but they also showed that they regarded those below them in the hierarchy as potentially incompetent, requiring constant scrutiny.

Menzies Lyth deduced that the organisation had set up a system to defend against the most powerful anxiety in nursing—to be responsible for a patient's death. An environment had been created in which any mistake, from leaving air bubbles in a syringe to failing to put proper hospital corners on the sheets, was treated as if it would have the same grave consequences. She pointed out that this functioned as one way of protecting nurses from being overwhelmed by the anxiety of (for example) filling a syringe. However, this had become so much part of the "mind" of the organisation, indeed of the profession itself, that it served merely to create a persecutory and repressive regime throughout the hierarchy—one mindlessly maintained without reflection.

Group relations conference: the structure

A group relations conference is set up as a temporary institution with the minimum infrastructure necessary to achieve its tasks. Each task will be defined and articulated so that it is clear to all participants. Structures will include both systems and roles. In this way the scene is set to study how these same structures, systems, and roles are used, misused, ignored, clung to, added to, or attacked by the conference membership. The assumption is that such behaviour will reveal the current anxieties within the membership. It is the demonstration in vivo of individuals' behaviours within the conference that provides the opportunity to learn from experience how they operate within group and institutional settings in the world outside. Experience has shown that these anxieties are not only to do with the actual tasks set in the programme, but also, and not surprisingly, to do with preoccupations that are brought into the conference by the membership. As Rice (1965, p. 19) put it, "Any institution considered as an open system can be defined by its imports and exports; that is, by the manifestation of its relations with its environment."

The primary task for a group relations conference may be defined by its title, which indicates to members the nature of its opportunities for learning—in particular, learning about the complex and interrelated nature of authority and leadership. The title for IGO Conferences is: "Group as a Whole Learning for Leadership, Authority and Organisation". The aim is to study the exercise of authority in the taking up of roles through the interpersonal, inter-group, and institutional relations that develop within the conference as an organisation in its context. The main export of a successful conference will be members who have gained in knowledge and experience of leadership, authority, and organisation.

How are the opportunities for this learning to be provided in the best possible way? Traditionally they have been achieved by a combination of experiential exercises and groupings through which the learning from the experience of the conference can eventually be applied to the member's normal work situation. Clearly, each element in the conference will have its own primary task. Opportunities to learn about leadership and authority will often arise at the boundaries of the various groupings and tasks. Most organisations have protocols that disguise the pressure at the boundaries, the "social systems" referred to earlier—but the group relations conference leaves these open. These areas are therefore those in which the need for negotiation and compromise occur. They will often include the following:

The plenary

The conference begins with a plenary session at which the director and the staff meet the membership. The director opens the conference and sets the agenda; this is usually a brief meeting, and its purpose is to provide a boundary, a formal threshold demarcating the line between ordinary life and the conference itself. This will be matched by a discussion group at the end of the conference that establishes the crossing back into the world outside the conference.

The small study groups (SSG)

These are small groups (usually eight members) given the task of using the experience of being in the conference and in their own particular small group to consider what is being learned about leadership and authority. It is conducted by one or sometimes two of the staff and tends to become the individual members' "home base", both in a literal and in an emotional sense (see Chapter 3).

The large-study-group (LSG) exercise

This is usually convened by two members of staff (traditionally the director and another) in which the whole conference, members and staff together, are invited to consider the experience of being at this particular conference. The large-group exercise occurs on day two (see Chapter 4).

The inter-group (IG) event

This provides an opportunity for the membership to create smaller groups of their own making, to study further the issues they find arising in the conference, which may also include personal issues. Staff are available to provide consultation to this process. They are usually available in the various rooms that constitute the territory of the conference. Often two consultants remain available in the plenary area, which becomes the place where groups can arrange to meet together (see Chapter 5).

The review and application group (RAG)

These are arranged at the end of each day, and provide an opportunity for members to bring issues from their own work to be thought about together with the group, assisted by a consultant (see Chapter 6).

Staff roles

Staff are essentially consultants to the process of carrying out the various tasks. At different times they will be available to some or all of the membership. They are expected to explore the unconscious dynamics that seem to be affecting the behaviour and the attitudes of the membership to whom they are consulting. As well, there is a hierarchy: the director manages the conference and has spent much time organising it beforehand together with the associate director and the administrator. The staff group meet before, during, and after each working day of the conference. They use their own experience including feelings, impulses, and dreams—as source material to facilitate their understanding of the dynamics of the conference.

The four-day IGO conference

Although history, tradition, and structure are important, they do not in themselves convey the intensity and emotional force of the actual experience. Each conference will be unique, and if the consultants are able to contain their own anxiety for long enough, they may—as becomes evident in any grouping—begin to see a pattern in the comments from the membership.

They may choose to point this out. Having said that, it may take the entire period of the conference to understand the unconscious preoccupations at any depth.

The rationale for its design

The above are the elements that make up the theoretical base for group relations conferences. To them is added the rationale for the design. Organisations tend to create systems that protect members from the raw experience of anxiety consequent upon engagement in the organisation's primary task. The best way, therefore, to learn about the pressures that force members to take up these defensive positions in the various workplaces is to create a setting that will provide some of the pressures without the actual consequences that might follow in the workplace itself. Thus, a group relations conference offers a direct experience of being in a group, in an organisation, with a task, but without the usual structures that shield participants, to a greater or lesser extent, from their raw emotional reactions.

A group relations conference defines itself as a temporary institution. It limits its own structures to the absolute minimum in order to accomplish its own primary task: that of providing a place in which issues of organisational defences, leadership, and authority may be studied in vivo. It is the absence of the "ordinary" structures that creates such a unique experience. Anyone who has ever been to such a conference will never forget the sense of confusion, excitement, raw feeling, and urge for structure that possesses him. Often the first things that members talk about are the way that there have been "mistakes" in the organisation, or in the structure, of the conference. Essentially the membership is complaining that the conventional structures of ordinary organisational life are absent. Instead, the conference provides alternative structures, which I describe below.

To summarise: groups tend to defend themselves against the anxiety that is a normal accompaniment of an organisation's primary task by moving into states of mind that Bion described as basic assumption modes (see Chapter 3). Individual members of the group tend to be drawn into familiar roles through their own personal valency. Defensive structures based on these basic assumption modes become fixed in organisations in a way that can be described as social systems. The nursing hierarchy described by Menzies Lyth based its functioning upon a "dependency" culture, in which "incompetence" was projected downwards in the hierarchy while "authority" was projected upwards.

Sometimes these structures are formalised within the infrastructure of the organisation, as was the case in that particular hospital.

By contrast, the group relations conference pares down organisational structures to the absolute limit, so that the members have a direct experience of the pressures on them to create structures that will apparently reduce anxiety. It is these same structures that can often make organisations dysfunctional. Learning derives through the actual experience of these pressures impacting on the individual, drawing him into dysfunctional activity; and this is followed by the chance to examine these same processes and their consequences within the conference itself.

The role of the consultant

In this brief discussion, I describe something of the approach that the consultant in a group relations conference might take, where the most important messages are conveyed unconsciously. As Freud wrote, "It is a very remarkable thing that the unconscious of one human being can react upon that of another, without passing through the conscious" (Freud, 1915e, p. 193). He also gave this instruction to those who would work psychoanalytically: the consultant "must turn his own unconscious like a receptive organ towards the transmitting unconscious of the patient [in this instance, members]" (Freud, 1912e, pp. 115–116).

In his roles, the consultant allows this process to happen. Helped by his own process of self-reflection, and experience as a member, from which he has come to recognise his own valencies, he monitors his emotional and psychological state for signs that an unconscious connection has occurred. Both continuous professional development and experience help one to learn how to use this information: including the fact that it is a mistake to take the conscious element of a primarily unconscious communication as the sum total of the communication itself. The consultant has first to allow an unconscious processing to occur within him so that, at some point, an idea will emerge. This is what Bion called the "selected fact". At that point the consultant will have to come to a view as to how to use this information in a way that the group can actually understand and which will further the work—that is to say, will be in the service of the task.

It is the task that distinguishes the role of group consultant: it does so not only in terms of how to use information that is conveyed both consciously and unconsciously, but also in terms of how to use the self. In group relations, the self of the consultant is available to the group as a screen on which to project material from the intrapsychic world. This might be emotions or ideas that the members cannot manage for themselves, or it might be aspects of significant people from his past that remain alive in his inner world at the moment. The task here is to enable the group to become aware of the way that he constructs and then views the outside world and the people in it to match his own unconscious expectations, phantasies, and beliefs.

The task of the consultant in a group relations situation is to expose the way that the group and the individual in it are managing feelings and ideas stirred up by the very business of processes going on in the room that make them anxious about working together. It is important to acknowledge that such things almost always preoccupy study groups. Yet the trick is not to assume that the same interpretation that applied in the last conference (or even earlier in the same conference) is apposite at this particular point.

The overall aim is to further members' knowledge and capacity for integrating thinking and feeling as they explore their experiences as members of the various groups. This integrative process which involves recognising, accepting, and appreciating one's own emotions, along with acquiring an intellectual understanding of their derivations and effects, is a fundamental component of the learning achieved in a group relations setting and is essential for understanding the dynamics of group behaviour in the "here and now". The focus will always be on learning at a group-as-a-whole level.

Our concept of how one comes to recognise and understand the unconscious dynamics that occur in groups is central to the structure and content of the learning situation. We define three learning goals:

(1) Improving the ability to observe what is happening at an overt level
(2) Improving the ability to identify the nature of one's own internal experience
(3) Being able to analyse how these two sets of data, in turn, may shed light on the covert processes taking place.

This involves learning about group processes by working at three levels—and linking all the information we gather thereby:

(1) What we see—the nonverbal cues that other group members give us, and the unconscious process of members' seating that informs us
(2) What we hear—what members of the group say, and what is the meaning of what they say for the group at this time
(3) What we feel—being in touch with one's own emotional feelings and open to the emotional experience of other group members.

Thus, by example, when the consultant enters the room, he may notice that there are several women sitting together, which may indicate that there is a gender issue in the group. Then listening to what the members are talking about, he may realise they are talking about how women are treated in their workplace; not least, the consultant will be in touch with his feelings and realise if he is feeling angry. Putting it all together the consultant may interpret that "the women are angry because the men in the group are treating them badly".

This is a first step and refers to describing or commenting on what behaviours are actually taking place in the group. For example, "Group members are fighting among themselves." An observation of this sort may be correct, but it adds little to what group members are capable of seeing for themselves. More subtle observations, such as, "Certain group members never look at each other," may have greater value.

Partial linking is the use of a "because" clause in connecting what the group is doing with what its behaviour may signify. It can take the form of observing a sequence of interactions that suggest an underlying dynamic not yet noticed by the group; for example: "The group keeps interrupting one of its members, which suggests that the group is unwilling or unable to listen to what certain members have to say." Alternatively, the link could be between the group's behaviour and the personal experiences of the consultant: "It feels as though the anger shown by the group towards one of its members is in fact anger intended for the consultant."

Understanding at this level connects all of the key components of interpretation: what the group is doing, how the consultant feels, and why. It starts with the self and with being in touch with the experience one is having. It provides a "because" clause that supports the link between oneself and the group. It connects feeling with thinking, either implicitly or explicitly. It has an almost intuitive quality, flowing between oneself and the group, in which one becomes an extension of the group. "I find myself experiencing a sense of alienation similar to that of the group member who, having taken on the role of outcast, keeps other members safe from having to deal with such feelings."

The pressing forward of this methodology is initially in the hands of the consultants. What follows is certainly not a prescription but my thoughts around this role.

First, the relatedness between the consultant and a group is one focus of study. The consultant interprets from his role perspective. Whether that is perceived and experienced as having more power than that of the members is open to examination. He interprets and formulates working hypotheses about the social processes, conscious and otherwise, that he understands to be present in the group.

Transference phenomena are part of the data. But he is part of that configuration in the room even though he is not in the group and not in the role of a member. If he becomes a member, the consultant function is lost which is sedulously to pursue the primary task. Yet the data from which the interpretation is derived are his experience of being pulled into membership on the one hand and extruded into limbo on the other.

Second, I sometimes explain to myself that the task of a consultant is a maieutic one in that he is helping members to realise their interpretations of the situation; in short, to exercise their authority to test realities. Clearly, the role is not didactic in the conventional sense but is to puzzle out from a role perspective what social phenomena are present in the situation, to form hypotheses, and to further learning. It is fashionable in educational settings to talk about raising the level of consciousness. This educational context includes just that, but it also provides a model, through behaviour, of how one gets in touch with unconsciousness. This is part of the conditions that the consultant provides to enable members to undertake these tasks for themselves. Just as for the workgroup leader who is in touch with the primary task, there will be continual attempts to seduce the consultant into a membership role and preferably one which satisfies the primitive wishes of the members. But if this happens, transference and countertransference feelings will be removed from the situation and the aim of understanding the nature of authority will disappear.

There is, third, a necessity that the consultant lead the group into problem areas for himself or herself in his role in relation to the members with whom he is working. At the same time, he needs to understand for himself or herself the experience of containment, the ability to allow the members to "be" in their terms. The boundary between these two is always puzzling, just as are the limits of certainty and uncertainty, chaos and order, which are all personally defined.

Fourth, the consultant is working with his subjectivity and attempting to use himself or herself as an instrument in the situation. The internal disentangling of what is being projected into the consultant and what is already there, having been introjected from his own past experiences, is a continual private task for the consultant. He needs to be able to work out, for example, how much uncertainty he owns and how much he is projecting on to the group when he leads into new areas of exploration by offering hypotheses. It is for this reason, among others, that those who direct group relations conferences should have always undergone an advanced training in small-group processes, and have a good understanding of self, through self-reflection. And they should attempt to recruit staff for working at conferences who will have psychoanalytic skills to bring to bear. To do otherwise is, to my mind, irresponsible.

Fifth, the consultant frames working hypotheses and interpretations on the basis of his experience in the role. These two terms are used interchangeably though it would be better if only the former were used. A working hypothesis is the social science equivalent of an interpretation which I tend to see as being a more appropriate tool for explicating interpersonal relationships.

The working hypothesis is a sketch of the reality of a situation to be either elaborated or erased and replaced by another sketch. The working hypothesis is always an approximation; valid and reliable at a particular point in time of the relationship between members of a grouping in a conference and the consultant or consultants. Reality, as I have said earlier, is construed subjectively. In the course of his personal development the individual has established a set of assumptions as to what constitutes reality and has organised his behaviour in relation to collective definitions of that reality. These assumptions and recipes for conduct give meaning to the individual's life. As important, they give some protection from fear and uncertainty. A working hypothesis, therefore, should normally be directed at the space between the members and the consultant, not directed at a particular member. If it is in the space between, so to speak, the member's freedom to work or not with the hypothesis is preserved. Then he knows that what he decides is on his authority.

The interpretation

We are indebted to Pierre Turquet (1974) who suggests that the interpretation usually creates a healthy pause where thinking and examining take place. The interpretation has put people in touch with the here and now and releases certain phenomena that happen in the pause. Often members speak individually and closer to the task after an interpretation.

The interpretation has a certain content. So has the pause. It is important to observe closely the fact of the content of the interpretation. This gives usually clear information to the leader of what forces are in operation in the group and in the members. In the work-group situation, the content of the interpretation is clearly used for further efforts to tackle the task. The content of the pause that emerges after the interpretation should show this.

Turquet also pointed to the necessity for providing evidence for an interpretation, what I refer to as asking the question, Why?—what he called the "because clause".

The "because clause" in the interpretation is very important because it is "out of time" and emphasises a long span of time of the group life, and it gets at the repetition compulsions of the members of the group since it reveals the past and the motives operating which were, before the interpretation, out of touch with the here and now. The past, so to say, has to be differentiated from the here and now so that unrealistic historical motives can be given up. It is also the way and method whereby the interpreter is exposing his own sense of reality and his understanding of what is going on at any moment. Thus, he also, as it were, tests his own sense of reality. Often new ideas flow into the here and now after the "because clause" has been mentioned. The "because clause" in the interpretation differentiates the past motives from the present and thus, as it were, cuts off the repetition compulsion where the individual tries to repeat past history. When the leader takes this historical motive into the current reality, he exposes it and can release the group to work more accurately on the actual task without the past interfering.

Ideally, members can internalise this mode of working and exercise their authority to interpret on the basis of their experience.

As we have seen, in relation to technique, for Bion the approach was always one in which the sole activity of the consultant was to make interpretations of the phenomena in the group as these developed. For this reason, Bion avoided any reference to individual psychopathology, seeing it as destructive to the experience of the basic group. Behind this was his conviction that any learning the members might get from the group rested upon them becoming more able to recognise themselves as being torn between the pull of the basic assumption group and their membership of the work group, which represented their ego functioning.

In IGO groups today, we do not attempt to follow Bion to the letter by avoiding all reference to aspects of the individual's behaviour. We may on occasion address them directly, while often linking them to an aspect of group process. The member, however, needs his individual problems to be known and acknowledged by the consultant; if the consultant restricts herself to group interpretations of any kind— our experience is that it can lead to the individual feeling abandoned or neglected. Activity deriving from the basic assumptions is addressed in its most specific forms as and when it starts to impede work-group functioning: an obvious example would be the kind of "flight" represented by members repeatedly arriving late, representing an attack on (a fight with) the learning process. Nevertheless, our approach to interpretation remains by and large "group centred": that is, centred on noticing and responding to the common themes, both conscious and unconscious—as they arise and cohere in the group and on the elucidation of the group's primitive and infantile anxieties.

Despite this apparent clarity, a common preoccupation among less experienced consultants is how and when to interpret at the level of the whole group while also attending to the learning of the individuals present. For example, training consultants often describe an uneasy feeling that they are "getting it wrong" when they fail in their observations and interpretations to take account of the group as a whole. The consultant will recognise that each individual in the group wants, and needs, his specific problems to be addressed, but feels at fault when responding too directly to the individual—particularly when it is not obvious to the consultant what the conscious and unconscious relevance may be for the group as a whole. In the staff meetings, the consultant may describe feeling that others in the group are being overlooked or that each individual is left jealously waiting for "his turn", as if there is a fantasy that each is receiving individual learning in the group. Conversely, when the consultant attempts to help the group through comments that address the whole group's functioning, he is often left feeling that his sincere attempts to do so now lead to a situation in which all the members in the group feel deprived or even provoked by him.

Clearly, it is a mistake to regard an "individual interpretation" as just that. A thoughtful interpretation to one individual may have far-reaching effects and relevance to others in the group. Indeed, in more socially withdrawn and anxious individuals, the therapeutic process often begins in cautiously observing and finding personal meaning for themselves in other members' responses to interpretations. Moreover, it is clear that an individual's problem is almost always a problem for the whole group in some way: either because he is the spokesperson for the underlying group conflict or because, as part of the group, he is an inherent part of the group's character. If this is kept in mind, the interpretation is more likely to feel as though it belongs and can be owned by the other members too.

The conflict regarding whole-group vs individually directed interpretation goes to the heart of the tension for the consultant in the group who wishes to help the individual but is in two minds as to whether this is best done by seeing the individual as primary to the group or secondary to it and in need of help with his hatred of a "groupish" nature.

Notwithstanding this general trend, an important contribution from Bion to groups comes from his work on the role of projective identification in groups. In the "Re-view", he suggests that most interpretations, and among them the most important, have to be made on the strength of the consultant's own emotional reactions. He says:

> It is my belief that these reactions are dependent on the fact that the analyst in the group is at the receiving end of what Melanie

Klein (1946) has called projective identification, and that this
mechanism plays a very important role in groups. ... The analyst
[in this case, consultant] feels he is being manipulated so as to
be playing a part, no matter how difficult to recognize, in some-
body else's phantasy ... (Bion, 1961, p. 148)

He concludes:

I believe ability to shake oneself out of the numbing feeling of
reality that is a concomitant of this state is the prime requisite
of the analyst [in this case, consultant] in the group: if he can
do this he is in a position to give what I believe is the correct
interpretation, and thereby to see its connection with the previous interpretation, the validity of which he has been caused to
doubt. (Bion, 1961, pp. 148–149)

In the second of the two clinical examples that follow, the importance
given to an understanding of the emotional responses of the consultant
in these terms will be evident. We use our experience, understanding,
and training in individual psychoanalysis to give us a greater appreciation of the unconscious primitive level in relation to both the individual
and the functioning of the whole group.

The normal way of constructing interpretations is, for example, "The
group is mobilising (an individual) as a flight leader." However, where
an individual has a strong valency, I might add, "and you (individual)
don't need to be mobilised, you can stop yourself being mobilised." In
this way, we give primacy to the group interpretation, but also interpret
to the individual.

In his final "Re-view", Bion (1952) attributes more power to the work
group than appears evident earlier in his text. He goes as far as to say
that in the long run, the work group usually triumphs over the basic
assumptions or succeeds in working in harmony with them. He con-
trasts this point of view with that of Le Bon who claims that "the masses
have never thirsted after truth" (1895). He then goes on to suggest that
the function of the specialised work group (he quotes the Church or the
Army) is to manipulate the basic assumption so as to prevent obstruc-
tion of the work group.

The consultant's tools

Thus far, I have concentrated a great deal on Bion's important work on basic assumptions. However, there is a need to understand other important matters which I now turn to. The consultant's tools in group relations are based upon a psychoanalytic understanding of human development and behaviour.

The consultant is enabled in his work through an understanding of the phenomena of the existence of unconscious mental processes, including unconscious communication between all group members, together with the mechanisms of defence against mental pain, or anxiety in particular, the mechanisms of splitting, projection and introjection, which are fundamental to group life. These are:

- Unconscious primitive processes
- The Oedipus complex
- Transference, and countertransference
- The concept of containment
- Projective identification

The understanding of these unconscious mental phenomena is conveyed to the group by the consultant via interpretations. However, the consultant is not providing a seminar on group dynamics, and interpretations are used only when the group is stuck, unable to do the work of understanding for itself. They follow the members' material rather than leading it and are expressed in plain language, with economy and simplicity. There should be no hint of reproach, of the "shoulds" and "should not haves" of the consultant's superego, no judgemental interpretation, although the members may experience interpretations as being judgemental.

Mechanisms of defence

From the beginning of life, the infant struggles to defend his own mental functioning against excesses of anxiety, which would interfere with mental development. The earliest and thus most primitive mechanisms used for these purposes are spontaneous, unconscious, and universal. Splitting refers to the infant's capacity to distinguish between good (pleasurable) and bad (unpleasurable) experiences, and to create a split between the agents felt to be responsible for each. Thus, although it is one and the same mother who is usually implicated in both kinds of experience, the infant separates the "good" mother, for whom the child feels love, from the "bad" mother, who is hated. A gradual and painful integration of these two versions of the mother begins to be possible later on within the first year of life, although human beings tend to have a lifelong struggle with this process in all important relationships. Is the group consultant who does not answer members' questions a consultant who is considered to be good because she is seen by the members as not encouraging dependency, or a bad consultant because she would not respond to the members' difficulties, one who can be turned away from and dismissed in anger and contempt?

Primitive mental activity

We go through certain crucial periods in our development that are created in, and characteristic of, the relationships we have been in and are still in. The course taken by these relationships forms the background psychologically for later relationships we might enter into. The early object relationship with the mother is imbedded in our unconscious, just like the oedipal relationships. Relationships with siblings form part of the basis of what we carry with us of conscious and unconscious traces in connection with jealousy and envy. In these relationships, we have learnt quite a lot about competition, collaboration, solidarity, and the field of tension between hate and love.

The paranoid–schizoid (regressive) position

In the earliest days of our existence the infant is engaged in what is referred to as primitive mental activity. At this stage of life this is a disorganised world and when as a child we are suffering from frustration and anxiety we respond in very primitive ways. When other people interfere with the child's desires things are simply experienced by the child as "good" or "bad" depending on the perceived experience. This is a "black and white" world where grey does not exist, and this is the most natural way of dealing with matters at the earliest stages of emotional development. Where other people are experienced as providing satisfaction of desires they are experienced as "good"; and, no matter that it is the same person who at another moment is perceived as thwarting the satisfaction of desires, they will be experienced as "bad". These views of black and white may be arrayed in the primitive manifestations of love and hate. At this stage of life, the infant is simply unable to distinguish other than at the level of black and white.

The defences that people employ when operating from the regressive position are, inevitably, fragmenting. Unwanted bits of experience, painful feelings, and despised parts of the self are split off and evacuated elsewhere when splitting, projection, and projective identification are relied upon to manage at that end of the spectrum of defences. The legacy of the paranoid–schizoid process is scapegoating; stalemated group splits; emotionally and intellectually disabled people; restricted collaborative ability across important boundaries; hateful, abusive, and paranoid authority relations; and an inability to understand immediate tasks in ways that allow people to link them to wider purposes. If consultants regress and end up, out of role, consulting in this mode there will be no hope of containment.

Regression in adult life

In regard to regression, to what we refer to as the paranoid–schizoid position, people cope with intense anxieties and threatening fears by relying on the more rudimentary, primitive end of the defensive spectrum, employing principally splitting, projective identification, and idealisation. This, in turn, leads to patterns of thought and experience characterised by blame, scapegoating, idealisation, persecution, and other distorted perceptions. When operating from this mode, the ability to engage in interpersonal relations is seriously compromised. Concrete thinking leads to rigidity, a loss of creativity, and polarisation which hampers the capacity to integrate differences and to collaborate.

The depressive (progressive) position

As opposed to the negative actions that emanate from the regressive position, as children we progress to what is technically known as the "depressive position" (also known as the progressive position). At this position we come to understand that our mother can be both good and bad, that the same person is capable of both being kind and caring and being harsh and neglectful. This is a considerable advance because the progressive position enables the integration of objects (different views, different groups, or different people), learning from experience, and the development of abstract thought, thus facilitating collaboration and transcendence in interests beyond our own survival and protection. While faced with the difficulties associated with projections into subgroup members which may be difficult to bear, it is vital for the members to develop a capacity for working in the depressive position.

Klein called the constellation of anxieties and defences around loss and grief the depressive position. She characterised the depressive position as a nodal point of development, first established in infancy and reactivated every time the person is faced with similar states of mind as in mourning. In developmental terms, Klein described the depressive position as a state of mind in which the baby experiences depressive feelings which reach a climax just before, during, and after weaning. It is melancholia in statu nascendi. The object which is being mourned is the mother's breast and all that the breast and the milk have come to stand for in the infant's mind: namely, love, goodness, and security. All these are felt by the baby to be lost, and lost as a result of his own uncontrollable, greedy, and destructive phantasies and impulses against the mother's breasts (Klein, 1940, p. 148).

Klein hypothesised that, when hungry, the baby hallucinates or conjures up in the mind a breast full of milk. But if for whatever reason the breast does not appear or the baby cannot feed, then the image of an angry or withholding breast will be created. At this stage the baby will scarcely be able to imagine the mother as a separate person, but instead will omnipotently imagine the state of her body to be a product of his own feelings and impulses. He will therefore believe the breast has become angry or withholding as a response to his own hatred, aggression, or greed.

In the depressive position the predominant mood is one of pining for the lost loved object (mother's breast and all it represents) and sorrow over the loss. Pining for the lost object implies dependence on it, and this can become an incentive to preserve and repair it.

But dependence on others can also be feared, as it will bring about the same experience of loss and disillusion. The leading anxiety is that hatred will overcome love, that one's loved object will be damaged by one's anger and hatred occasioned by the experience of separation and loss. The main defences against such depressive anxieties are manic in nature. Feelings of loss or guilt can be denied through a sense of triumph or control over the loved object. Or an attitude of manic reparation can be adopted; for example, expressed in an overprotective and sentimental attitude towards the loved object, which is based on a fear of one's own aggression and of retaliation by the loved object rather than genuine concern.

Klein called the constellation of such feelings and anxieties the paranoid–schizoid position, which she envisaged as a counterpart to the depressive position. In the paranoid–schizoid position it is the very existence of the person and the world which is at stake, as persecutory and paranoid anxieties dominate. The leading anxiety is that one's hatred of the loved object, occasioned for instance by inevitable frustration around feeding at the breast, will result in retaliation and persecution by this loved object, which will have been transformed into a hating object. The intensity of the persecution experienced is such that the infant feels in danger of being annihilated. The main defences employed against this persecutory anxiety are both more primitive and more powerful than those of the depressive position, and involve the splitting and/or evacuation of experience. Experiences are split into good and bad, with a rigid distinction between them so that the bad cannot contaminate the good and all the good will be lost. Another way of controlling the bad is to evacuate it into the world outside, where it is felt to take over and control people, leaving all the goodness inside oneself (this defence was called projective identification by Klein).

Klein saw the depressive and paranoid–schizoid positions as both developmental and structural concepts. She envisaged the infant initially passing through the paranoid–schizoid position, around the first few months of life, and then, if all went well, moving towards the depressive position. However, she was careful to call these constellations of anxieties and defences "positions", rather than "stages", as she wanted to emphasise that they remain as permanent patterns in the mind throughout.

The importance of progressive and regressive positions

It is important to understand the effects of these two positions on consultants in their attempts to exercise power. Should they fail to exercise self-containment and revert to a regressive mode of consulting, all trust will disappear and phantasy and hatred will be the order of the day. It will be a stand-off between "us" (the members) and "them" (the consultants) that is unmovable and preventing the creativity and willingness required to create learning. If consultants can stay in the progressive position, no matter what members do, and consistently and persistently approach all situations by staying in touch with reality, this will result in creativity and working towards the development of new learning.

Denial

Denial means that an important aspect of emotional reality is ignored, or one aspect of these ambivalent feelings is cut off from awareness altogether. This leads to idealisation of, for instance, the consultant or, conversely, to denigration. The consultant whose word is divine, who is never mistaken, is as much a product of denial as is the creation of a consultant who is felt to be a purveyor of rubbish—useless, clueless, and worthless.

When individuals are faced with extreme anxiety, they use an unconscious defence mechanism such as denial whereby they split off their unbearable thoughts and feelings and deny the reality. As the name suggests, denial is the unconscious process of disowning some aspect of a conflict, with the result that the conflict no longer appears to exist. Denial refers to aspects of a situation that the person does not want to perceive. There is a denial of the external data. Faced with really bad news that we find so unpleasant and so unbearable to our consciousness, we disown it by the unconscious process of denial.

Projection

Projection refers to the tendency to split off and deny certain unwanted aspects of one's own functioning and then to perceive them as belonging to another. Although projection is an intrapsychic process the split-off attributes are deposited in an internal representation of someone other than the self, a host—and it is often followed by altered behaviour to the actual individual in question. When this behaviour succeeds in nudging the host into behaving in accordance with the projected phantasy, then the projection has become a projective identification. The host has, in turn, identified through introjection with what has been projected.

Projective identification

Projective identification is the lifeblood of human communication when non-insistent, fluid, and retractable, allowing others to retain an emotional life of their own. In excess, it is highly pathological, controlling, and exhausting, dominating and restricting the host's functioning as well as that of the projector—who loses aspects of his own ego's functioning through having projected them out and into others. It is the source of much distress and misunderstanding in intimate human relations, whether in the one-to-one setting, or in small or in large groups. Small-group settings offer an exceptional opportunity to see and eventually to come to understand this process in action.

I now want to show how the mechanisms of projective and introjective identification operate in linking individual and social behaviour. Projective identification is an important process that enables us to understand a wide range of group and organisational phenomena. Projective identification is a frequent occurrence between two or more persons or groups whereby one side projects certain unwanted mental contents onto and into another person or group, with a resulting alteration in the behaviour of the targeted object. It is not just a mechanism of projection since it also affects another person or group.

While projective identification is a defensive process in the sense of unconsciously serving to insulate the projector from an aspect of his experience, it is also a mode of communication in the sense that the feelings which are congruent with one's own inner image are induced in another, creating a sense of "being understood by or at one with the other". As various group members, subgroups, or organisational sectors come to symbolise or represent some unwanted aspect, they can serve as repositories for certain projected-out elements and are then induced to enact these feelings or phantasies. The often-observed patterns of role differentiation in which groups pressure a member into a needed role, and scapegoating, are comprehensible in terms of projective identification.

Projective identification refers to efforts by persons to rid themselves of certain mental contents by depositing unwanted feelings into another's feeling system. The first person wishing to get rid of an unwanted feeling treats the other as if they had or embodied the feeling state. The way in which the recipient of this process responds has an important impact on the experience of the sender. If the recipient simply enacts the role he is assigned, then a tacit, collusive agreement is established in which the original meaning of the unwanted feelings or fantasies is reinforced and the defence against thinking about them confirmed. It will be recalled that if we want to feel good about ourselves then "not me" has to be bad. We need the other to confirm we are not like that. Thus, the scapegoat takes on or accentuates the characteristics attributed to him and confirms the repugnance the others feel for that (disowned) aspect. Perhaps a member embodies the role assigned by the group, such as the rebellion leader.

More sophisticated defence mechanisms might include rationalisation, reaction formation, displacement, regression, and so on. These tend to be more influenced by cultural factors than are the primitive and universal defences described above.

Unconscious communication

Unconscious communication between individuals is not magic, nor is it some arcane piece of psychoanalytic superstition. It is a real phenomenon that the psychoanalytically trained consultant comes to recognise and make use of in the course of the work (and, indeed, in life in general). It is the fundamental process underlying the phenomena of projective and introjective identification and their manifestation in countertransference experiences. Only if the communication remains unconscious do countertransference phenomena come to exist, or the projective or introjective identifications succeed in controlling or affecting the functioning of their host, or target. Thus, it refers to communication by means of processes and mechanisms that often proceed subliminally and which have not yet been fully understood. Often, the deconstruction of something we called intuition or a hunch will reveal some of the processes underlying this phenomenon, which can be observed in any setting in which people come to know each other well and spend time together.

Thus, it affects those who live and work in close and prolonged proximity, as well as couples, families, consultants together with their members, and the members of group relations groups. Vision and hearing are involved, and with time, the micro-cues that are being responded to can be recognised. This is harder for humans to do with the sense of smell, but this also is powerfully implicated. Sometimes unconscious communication is manifested as having the same thought at the same moment. Often it is seen as the communication of mood and atmosphere and thus state of mind. Although these phenomena are universal among human beings, the exceptional feature of the group relations setting is that their existence may be acknowledged, spelled out, and understood between the implicated individuals.

The important questions for the consultant to hold in mind are: Why am I having this feeling or thinking this thought at this moment? Does it arise autonomously within me, or am I responding to something done/said/going on in the member or membership?

The need to disentangle and recognise the difference between something that arises autonomously within the consultant (from her own personal life) from something that is stirred up by a particular encounter with a particular member in a particular state of mind, is part of why an intensive advanced training for the consultant is crucial. Without it, the temptation to resort to, for example, the thought that the group is shutting me out today as a crude defence against the recognition of a personally cut-off state of mind can be powerful.

Transference and countertransference

Transference is the name given to specific phenomena deriving from early relationships, in which beliefs, moods, phantasies, states of mind, and ways of relating developed in relation to a number of important early figures come alive again in the here and now of the consultant relationship and are re-enacted within it. However, there need not be an idealisation of the capacity in either consultant or member to acknowledge the transference. A recognition of links with the past may clarify matters and improve vision, but on its own it will not necessarily help the member to change his functioning in the present. It is how the members employ the multiple and shifting bits of transference, all deriving from an assemblage of early relationships, that will determine the extent to which they can be helped to improve matters. For example, a paranoid or an eroticised transference may be so powerful and concrete as to make it impossible for the member to objectify and observe his own situation. An anorexic transference makes it very difficult for the patient to take in anything the group or the consultant has to offer. Less rigid transferences, or modes of relating, where the unconscious anxieties are not so great that the member cannot risk making contact with this new object, the consultant will shift and change over time. As these new objects become significant and eventually important to the individual member, he will take them inside (introject them), and this in itself will affect and modify the existing internal structures, and hence his object relations. The nature of the transference will shift and sometimes soften, and the reality of the external object come to be given more significance.

The converse, countertransference, is the name given to the moods, phantasies, and states of mind conjured up in the consultant through exposure to the powerful and often at first invisible transferences brought by the members in the group. An anorexic transference in members or in the group may evoke a rage in the consultant, linking with the helplessness of the original feeding parent watching his child starve. However, the consultant must be careful not to confuse the thoughts or feelings he has brought with him into the group with a genuine countertransference. Here we are reminded that the consultant needs to eschew (give up) all memories, thoughts, and desires before taking up his role as a consultant. Learning to use countertransference feelings and impulses stirred up in the consultant rather than enacting them is a lengthy and complex process; it is never foolproof.

Containment

The containing function is about noticing, receiving, and digesting primitive emotions, raw affect, incoherent states of mind in the group, and damaging interactions. This is a vital function for the role of consultant. Once digested, consultants need to take decisions about what and how to interpret.

Consultants need to understand that disturbances are necessary in periods of learning. Their psychological absence may signal splitting and unhealthy, rigid denial caused by overwhelming anxiety, which the group members perceive a consultant as too weak to handle—so they stop projecting, challenging, rebelling. A robust and healthy system will manage regression in the group and obtain much learning from it. Consultants must not ignore and must not deny or diminish it, otherwise they will be seen as fragile. Where the consultant fails in his task of providing containment it becomes impossible for the members to tolerate so much anxiety.

The group suffering these unbearable thoughts and feelings also splits off these feelings and may project them into another part of the group, usually another small study group or a subgroup of foreigners. In adult life we are able to understand that people are, for example, psychologically whole individuals who can be showing both "good" and "bad" ways of behaving. However, when we are faced with anxiety, particularly extreme anxiety, this may evoke in our unconscious much of our previous primitive experience. In these circumstances we may employ precisely the same defence. Splitting is frequently experienced in the group either by individuals or by subgroups. The needs of the members of the conference to use it in the struggle against anxiety can lead to the development of socially structured defence mechanisms, which appear as elements in the conference structure, culture, and mode of functioning.

Containment of these countertransferential thoughts and feelings, which means a thoughtful examination by the consultant of her own internal responses to the group, often provides important information about the shifting transferences and states of mind within the members. The consultant's capacity to hold on to the often disturbing and uncomfortable countertransferences evoked in her by the complex nature of the compound organism that is the group, without acting on these feelings, is an important feature of what is required of group relations consultancy. Through her struggle to process what has been stirred up in her by her members, she offers the members an auxiliary mind, one capable of bearing and dealing with some of what the members have been unable to manage.

The consultant is functioning in a way that can be compared to that of the mother in relation to the infant. Before the infant learns how to communicate wishes and needs in any way other than through a massive projection of them into the mother, the child relies upon the mother to recognise those feelings through her own identification with them. She has to be able to know what they are without becoming overwhelmed by them herself. If she is able to contain the infant's state inside herself, think about it, and respond helpfully, the infant will gradually become able to do this processing autonomously. Group consultants have to serve this exact same function for the group, coming to know something of the subterranean states and moods at work in it, reflecting on them, and responding helpfully. However, it is very rarely useful merely to tell the group what it is feeling. This will be experienced as pushing the feeling back at them in an admonitory way. The group needs to be helped to recognise its own state of mind, which helps the process of objectification, which, in turn, allows for an understanding of the multiple factors that have contributed to it. In this respect, a containing consultant can in the end be more helpful than one who is over-busily interpreting. The work is slower, but the effects are more durable.

The Oedipus complex

The Oedipus complex refers to the pattern of relationships between the child and his parents which shape the child's emotional, psychological, and sexual development. It is a way of thinking about how the child navigates a way through the complexities of needing to identify with his parents, that is, becoming like them while also separating from them, in effect being different from them. It is about the way the child makes sense of the difference between the sexes and between the generations. Freud thought the child negotiates the Oedipus complex in several stages. For the male child, his first love object is his mother, a love which starts with him feeding at her breast. But, said Freud, while the little boy loves his mother and desires to be close to her, he identifies and wishes to be like his father. For a time, these two relationships, love for mother and identification with father, proceed side by side. But at some point, perhaps due to an increase of intensity in his love for his mother, the boy comes up against a barrier. He is forced to acknowledge a reality of both generation and gender: that it is his father who has a prior claim on his mother, and stands in the way of him becoming too close, or acting like a lover to his mother. In the boy's mind the father has now become an obstacle, a rival for his mother's love.

This development marks the beginning of the Oedipus complex. The boy's identification with his father now takes on a hostile colouring. Together with his continuing admiration and love for his father as the person he wishes to emulate, the boy now wishes to get rid of his father in order to take his place and have his mother to himself. From now on the little boy's relationship with his father is ambivalent. This, then, is what Freud called the simple form of the Oedipus complex, so called because it is based on Sophocles' story of Oedipus, who killed his father and married his mother. Freud initially saw the little girl following a similar path, having to negotiate taking her father as a love object, and then encountering her mother as both an object of identification and as a rival for the father's affection. However, he then realised that the situation of the little boy and girl is not symmetrical, as both have the experience of the mother's love and attention from the beginning, expressed above all in the feeding relationship to the breast. The little boy continues taking his mother as his love object, whereas the little girl has to transfer her love for her mother onto the figure of her father before she enters the simple form of the Oedipus complex. For both the little boy and the little girl, then, this initial relationship with the mother plays a vital part in their readiness to enter into the Oedipus complex. However, the simple form of the Oedipus complex was a notional one for Freud, for in his view little boys and girls do not have a fixed gender identity. In his words they are psychically bisexual, that is, able to take on the behaviour and experience of both genders. The little boy, as well as loving his mother and having his father as both rival and object of identification, also loves his father and identifies with his mother. In a complementary way the little girl takes each parent as both love object and object of identification. So, for Freud, each child has to negotiate this constellation of object choices and identifications; this bisection of desire—I love my mother/father—with identity—I am like my mother/father—which forms the Oedipus complex in its complete form.

There is no predetermined outcome, as the child will go through the range of oedipal feelings (love, hate, jealousy, affection) and identifications with each parent before coming to a more fixed constellation. The way the Oedipus complex is negotiated will establish a template of relationships and states of mind which will serve as a backdrop to all of the growing child's future dealings with other people.

There is an implicit idea of successful or unsuccessful negotiation of the Oedipus complex. This has led some mental health professionals (more so in the past than today) to use the Oedipus complex in a reductionist and moralistic way as a justification of their own prejudices, notably in equating the successful outcome of treatment with the finding of a "correct" love object, that is, a heterosexual one. However, Freud considered the Oedipus complex as a much more subtle instrument, where it is the range of identifications and the quality of relationships rather than the simple choice of object which determines how successfully the Oedipus complex has been negotiated. For Freud a mark of the successful negotiation of the Oedipus complex is a person's ability to become independent of their parents. Much of the impetus for this comes from the child's inevitable frustration of his oedipal feelings (e.g. the little boy has to give up his possessive love for his mother as he is too small to really compete with father for her love), which pushes him to find satisfaction in other relationships. The drive and intensity of oedipal feelings, once turned away from the frustrating parental figures, is then available to be used in other areas of the child's life, for example, in intellectual or artistic development (Freud called this process sublimation, which he saw as an essential part of an individual's development). Inhibition and impotence, both in relationships and achievements in life, are signs of a person who has remained stuck at some point in their negotiation of the Oedipus complex.

In describing the Oedipus complex and the depressive/paranoid-schizoid modes of experience separately, the question arises as to how these two conceptual frameworks articulate with each other. In order to negotiate the various stages of the Oedipus complex, the individual would need to have developed sufficiently so that other people are not seen simply as extensions of oneself but as existing in their own right, and also capable of making relationships with others from which one might be excluded. Now this is one of the defining features of the depressive position. In other words, the capacity to negotiate the Oedipus complex, and the capacity to have experiences in the depressive mode, are ways of describing a similar psychological and emotional constellation from different perspectives.

The paranoid–schizoid position is more linked to difficulties prior to negotiating the Oedipus complex. Indeed, where paranoid–schizoid experiences dominate the picture, an oedipal structure may seem to be entirely lacking.

This particular complex of relationships with our primary others is the basis not only of all our social relations but of the very structure of our minds and modes of thinking. An unsatisfactory working out (it is never complete) of the oedipal (triangular) situation and its many derivatives will lead to difficulties in developing the full use of the mind, and a full capacity to engage in relations with others. Group relations provides a rich field for observation of the actuality of the shifting triangular networks within it for everyone within the group, not only for the consultant. Moreover, in a group relations group, licence to understand and to state out loud the implications of these observations is unrivalled. The Oedipus complex is so fundamental to our mental life, both conscious and unconscious, that its importance cannot be overstated. Consultants who are unaware of its workings in themselves are unlikely to be capable to helping their groups with the many and complex manifestations of it in group life. The oedipal relationships are associated with attachment—"the progress of the love affair"—with the parent of the opposite sex, and, at the same time, it is the first important experience of having a rival. It is therefore the first relationship where we experience there is also a risk associated with strong emotional relationships.

The relevance of the Oedipus complex in group relations may concern a member's separation anxiety and the defences against it, the projection of aggression and resultant experiences of being persecuted from without, depression and mourning and a member's efforts at reparation, castration anxiety and the defences against it.

CHAPTER 3

The small study group (SSG)

There has long been increasing understanding of the behaviour of individuals and of groups. But knowing about group processes and human behaviour does not necessarily mean that use can be made of the knowledge and understanding. Moreover, knowledge, let alone its effective use, cannot generally be gained from reading, lectures, or books. Both the acquisition of knowledge and learning how to use it require direct experience. The aim of group relations conferences described in these chapters is therefore to enable the members to learn, through direct experience, how to work with others as individuals and as members of the groups to which they belong. The conferences provide opportunities for members to experience what forces are brought to bear on them when they take roles that require them to lead others, and what forces they bring to bear on those who lead them. They learn what it feels like to be, and how to behave as, both leaders and followers, and they experience the conflicts that arise in themselves and in others when they take, or are mobilised into, these roles.

The assumption is made throughout these chapters that individual behaviour is affected by unconscious forces, and, as a corollary, that individuals and groups of individuals always behave in ways that are not wholly explicable in terms of their rational and overt intentions. It is also assumed that, in any group or institution, unconscious motives affect the decisions that are taken; that any committee meeting, for example, has both a written and an unwritten agenda and it is the unwritten agenda that takes up so much time; and that jealousies, guilt, anxiety, and undisclosed and often unrecognised struggles for power or authority have a profound effect on the acceptance or rejection of solutions to apparently straightforward problems. In short, it is assumed that intelligent human beings, whether acting alone or as members of groups, do not behave stupidly, or in ways that are manifestly opposed to their declared interests without cause, and that understanding of the denied or repressed causes can make a major contribution to the solution of problems of leadership.

By small group is meant the "primary" or "face-to-face" group. It must consist of more than one individual and must not contain more members than can sustain continuous and close personal relationships. The most relationships that have to be sustained in groups is twelve. Any number larger than that is likely to split into subgroups. In the groups described in these chapters, twelve is the maximum number that is used for small-group learning; in practice it is likely to be about ten.

In the IGO model of group relations conferences, the small study group (SSG) is the task of the first day. The task of the small study group is to provide opportunities to learn about interpersonal relationships in small face-to-face groups. The primary task is to study the behaviour of the group, as a group, as it happens.

Aims and structure

The overall aim is to further members' knowledge and capacity for integrating thinking and feeling as they study their experiences as members of a small study group. This integrative process which involves recognising, accepting, and appreciating one's own emotions, along with acquiring an intellectual understanding of their derivations and effects, is a fundamental component of the learning achieved in a group relations setting and is essential for understanding the dynamics of group behaviour in the "here and now". The focus is on learning at a group-as-a-whole level.

A group relations conference limits its own structures to the absolute minimum in order to accomplish its own primary task: that of providing a place in which issues of organisational defences, leadership, and authority, may be studied in vivo. It is the absence of the "ordinary" structures that creates such a unique experience. The best way for members to learn about the pressures that force people to take up defensive positions in the various workplaces is to create a setting that will provide some of the pressures without the actual consequences that might follow in the workplace itself.

The group relations conference, therefore, pares down organisational structures to the absolute limit, so that the members have a direct experience of the pressures on them to create structures that will apparently reduce anxiety. It is these same structures that will inevitably result in dysfunctional behaviour. Learning derives through the actual experience of these pressures impacting on the individual, drawing him into dysfunctional activity; and this is followed by the chance to examine these same processes and their consequences within the conference itself.

As consultants it is vital for containment that will enable learning that we ensure that we always stay on task, provide a secure territory, and always work to time—and understand the importance of doing so. Because of the anxiety experienced by the members, the consultant will frequently become the object of projections. Something I learnt when I first became an organisational and a group relations consultant was that negative projections were not too difficult to reject; however, positive projections, for example, "the consultant is so clever", were more difficult because they were seductive. I learnt that when forms of idealisation were occurring, I needed to be very aware and not be seduced out of my role. To do so, for any reason, will result in a group being totally uncontained, and learning at an end.

This requires the consultant to prepare himself before taking up the consultant role. It means eschewing all memory, desire, and understanding that the consultant may have brought with them into the conference; and by self-reflection, identify and be able to control any form of performance anxiety. It is vital that the consultant is led by the group, that the consultant is working with whatever is happening in the group. To be influenced by stuff that he brings into the group is off task: no learning can take place.

There are, of course, things that we need to bring with us into the group; for example, knowledge of the consultant role and knowledge of work groups and basic assumption groups. Here, it is helpful to turn to the practical and theoretical learning provided by Bion; particularly his understanding regarding the emotional aspect of groups. But first I think it will be helpful to consider how our psychological development is reflected in the group.

Psychological development: the individual in the group

Groups are, of course, made up of aggregates of individuals. Is there such a thing as an individual who is not a member of a group of some kind? Over the hours, days, and weeks after birth, the baby's ego forms through the accretion of experience, both that which comes mainly from the environment and that which arises mainly from internal sources, around an internal nucleus containing the relationship with the primary caregiver, the source of life after birth. Some version, or versions, of that primary caregiver will be taken into the baby along with the milk and the care and protection the infant needs, both when these needs are satisfied and when they are not. The baby's own responses, feelings, and phantasies connected with these experiences, both good and bad, add swiftly to the growth of an internal world, which becomes increasingly populated by several different kinds of object—equally configured as good or bad arising out of the subtle interaction of experience, phantasy, and response that has given rise to them.

The complexity of this internal world increases rapidly as these internalised objects become organised in various ways of relating to each other. That primary group of three is the nucleus of the infant's developing internal world, his own internal group; the nucleus of the child's eventual mental processes, the oedipal configuration, basic to the processes of thought; and the nucleus of his social context, that which will eventually become his social world.

There are, then, two major tasks ahead for that baby, which is to say, every human infant. He has to develop as an individual, in touch with his own internal world: his impulses, phantasies, wishes, ideas, and feelings, whether pleasurable or unpleasurable, whether derived from and dominated by hate or derived from and expressive of love. As he contains the capacity for, at different times, both love and hate, he has to learn how to manage the balance. How much rage and hatred can be directed at his object, whom he also loves, before that object's capacity to go on caring for him is exhausted? How remorseful can he feel, and how capable is he of showing this in his behaviour when he has wounded or damaged the object? How much love, on the other hand, can he go on feeling for an object who ignores or maltreats him before his own capacity for loving is extinguished?

These are immensely complex questions. As organisational and group relations consultants, we deal with the consequences of these early processes in our daily consultancy work. As psychoanalytic group consultants we see them worked out in the to and fro of the interactions, often intense and sometimes explosive, between group members, and in the relation of the individual to the group itself. This is the second major task facing the developing child, and it continues into adolescence and throughout adulthood: the child has to learn how to become a member of a group, while retaining his particularity, his individuality, his capacity to think for himself or herself.

This is more easily said than done. To be a member of a group is to have to put into practice some of those earlier developmental steps to do with the balance between love and hate; to be able to hold back on personal aims and ambitions when the needs of the group require something other from each of its members. Bion (1992) described this process as a move from narcissism to socialism.

At the same time, we know that however ruthlessly narcissistic an individual might be, they are lost without the group. And, conversely, however deprived and damaged an individual may be, they can be helped, even rescued, by the group. We know that it is not enough for a mother to give her baby nutrition alone without the engaged and responsive relationship that should provide the context of that feeding. The feeding, though necessary, is insufficient in terms of creating a sentient being capable of recognising others as sentient, with minds of their own.

Feeding is not the same as love itself, and it will not engender the capacity to love in return. It is about survival and is, at its best, but one expression of love, which is about our relations with others. As do biologists, psychoanalysts and psychoanalytic consultants see the drive for relatedness to other members of our own species as primary, an intrinsic part of our make-up. It is as fundamental to our being—and to our well-being, our mental functioning, and to our very survival as human beings—as are the drives for food, shelter, warmth, and sex.

The emotional life of groups

Working with the emotional life of groups, Bion was amazed at the futility of group conversations: if judged by ordinary standards of social intercourse, groups are almost devoid of intellectual content, so he focused on the emotional charges underlying verbal exchanges rather than their contents. Drawing his hypothesis closer to his experience, Bion substituted desires for the needs of his original formulation of group culture as a function of the conflict between individual and group mentality. In the group mentality the individual finds a means of expressing the contributions which he wishes to make anonymously, and at the same time his greatest obstacle to the fulfilment of the aims he wishes to achieve by membership of the group.

Bion discovered that the group interaction can be categorised into three types of basic assumption, and an individual who contributes to the group mentality will feel uneasy whenever he thinks or acts in a way that does not accord with the basic assumption in play. Bion focused on identifying the types of basic assumptions to be found in groups. By the end of his research Bion was convinced that in all groups there is an interaction between two levels of emotional activity. One of these he calls the work group; the other he calls the basic assumption group. The category of work group describes only one aspect of mental activity (it does not describe the individuals constituting the group). All individual members of the group voluntarily cooperate with the necessary activities. All activity presupposes a contact with reality which requires respect for reality. As a consequence, the work group is characterised by its awareness of the dimension of time, and the need for progress. Characteristic of the work group are those features which Freud describes as characteristic of the ego.

Bion was concerned to identify those mental activities which impede, corrupt, or sometimes support the rational group process. They derive from powerful emotional states which push the faculty of judgement into second place. At first sight these activities seem rather chaotic, but they acquire a certain coherence when they are understood as manifestations of the basic assumption held in common by all members of the group. It is not that members of the group create a basic assumption and all else follows from this; rather that the emotional state exists first and the assumption follows from this. The work group requires an aptitude for collaboration with other participants. The basic assumption group, by contrast, is held together by an automatic and involuntary participation of its members. To account for this Bion uses the concept of valency as a description of an individual's readiness to enter into combination with a group in making and acting on basic assumptions. An individual without valency would no longer be human.

The basic assumption group does not recognise the passage of time, and understands little of whatever relates to time. It therefore rejects all processes of growth and development, which depend on changes in time, and in place of growth it offers the alternative of a feeling of increased vitality. This longed-for alternative to the group procedure is really something like arriving fully equipped as an adult fitted by instinct to know, without training or development, exactly how to live and move and have his being in a group.

Bion was preoccupied with two questions concerning basic assumption groups. The emotions associated with basic assumptions can be described in familiar terms, such as anxiety, fear, hatred, love. But these emotions affect one another when they are combined in a basic assumption. This means that anxiety, for example, as it is expressed in the dependence group, is different from its expression in the pairing group. The same holds true for other emotions and their combination. In a word, the important thing is not the presence of such and such a feeling, personal security to take one example, but the way in which it combines with others. The first question concerns the nature and origin of psychological combinations. Bion wonders why it is that emotions can combine with a tenacity and exclusivity characteristic of chemical reactions. There are no conflicts between the basic assumptions, and they can alternate easily within the same group. Conflict arises from the relationship between the basic assumption group and the rational (work) group. However, the emotional state associated with each of the basic assumptions excludes the emotions characteristic of the other basic assumptions. This leads Bion to his second question: What happens to the latent affects, the emotions belonging to the basic assumptions that are inactive in a group?

When a person joins a group, they try to identify themselves entirely with either the basic assumption or the rational structure. If a member identifies themselves with the basic assumption, they feel persecuted by what seems to them to be the arid intellectualism of the group (and especially interpretations). If the member identifies with the rationality of the group, they feel persecuted by internal objects. The emotional state of the group's basic assumption cannot be acceptable to all concerned. The group process can support individuals only in detaching themselves from everything they find bad. The feelings which an individual seeks in a group exist only in combination with other feelings which may be less desirable to them, or even strongly disliked by them. The group consultant should allow himself or herself to see all situations in a double psychological perspective.

Understanding group dynamics

Group dynamics refers to the processes that inevitably take place in groups, especially relatively closed or relatively stable groups, between members at all levels. An understanding of group dynamics is important for group relations consultants as it gives them a perspective on the group as a whole, helping them widen their focus to include more depth and perspective than the individual members and their histories on their own. Just as an individual has intensive therapy as a vital part of the therapist's training in the field of object relations, so an experience in a training group is a vital part of becoming a group relations consultant.

Task, territory, and time

The concepts of task, territory, and time provide a clear understanding of the importance that boundaries are essential. However, understanding why these factors are important is as necessary as knowing that they are part of the process. Above all, the three Ts, as they've become known, provide containment for the difficult task of learning.

Task, territory, and time are concerned with establishing the boundaries of the group, which need to be protected.

Task

The task of a group for recalling and recording memories, or making up a photograph album, is clear. The task of a group relations group is harder to spell out: studying the behaviour of the group as a group, as it happens, is an unfamiliar process. It is not surprising then that group members find the conference task difficult. However, the fact that the consultant stays in role is a key element in providing containment.

Territory

The external boundary between the conference and the outside world needs to be secure because it is, in one sense, part of what enables a collection of individuals with a task in hand to become a group. The role of the administrator is to secure the external boundary and to limit contact between members and outsiders during the working sessions.

The group takes place in the same room in each session, and at the stated times, and it is part of the consultant role to ensure that the room needs to be free of interruption from outside agencies. The consultant is also responsible for setting the correct number of chairs for the members and consultant(s), in a circle that best provides opportunities to learn about interpersonal relationships in small face-to-face groups. The task of setting the room extends to ensuring that the chairs are reset between sessions, including removing items of clothing and reading material from chairs. It is important that when the members return to the room they are presented with a cleaned-up room, a properly set circle, and nothing to indicate prior ownership of chairs. At the start of this new group, we need to see the way the members take up their seating.

Time

The boundary—both of territory and time—marks the edge between the inside and the outside, demarcating the membership of the group from the membership of the whole of the rest of the conference membership.

The group consultant's job is, among other things, to protect that boundary. Strangers, non-group members, will be excluded. In a Leicester conference, I was a small-group consultant when a member who was allocated to another group decided she wanted to be in my group. This was known to the conference director who told me that if she did join the group, I should push my chair out of the circle and tell the group that I could not consult to the group as I only had authority to consult to the named group. In other words, part of my role was to protect the boundary of the group.

When the group's time and space is protected, what goes on inside the group feels more solid, safe, and contained, allowing for the expansion of individual limits and boundaries. In the same way that there is a physical territory, there is also an emotional boundary in a learning group. What takes place within the group remains private to the members of that group. It is not taken outside. For example, members may try to engage group consultants in the break about something that has occurred. An important response is that "this is a matter for the group as a whole and needs to be discussed in the group".

The needs of task, territory, and time will exist throughout the duration of the conference. However, it will be important that the consultant makes it clear that the task will change, and the consultant's task may also change in the different conference events.

The first session

The usual first contribution is simply that of telling the members the task is "to study the behaviour of the group, as a group, as it happens". The members come into the conference with the normal knowledge and experiences that they have gained in the various organisations that they come from. Thus, there are expectations; for example, organisations tend to create systems that protect members from the raw experience of anxiety consequent upon engagement in the organisation's primary task.

The members are then left in the unusual situation of a group relations event that offers a direct experience of being in a group, in a conference, with a task, but without the usual structures that shield participants, to a greater or lesser extent, from the raw emotional experience. The conventional structures of ordinary organisational life are absent. Instead, the conference provides alternative structures, which I describe below.

A frequent response to this sense of confusion is the need for structure, whereby a member may be mobilised to express a form of their familiar way of behaving, to introduce themselves. During this process, they inevitably try to include the consultant, and find it strange when the consultant does not follow their behaviour by introducing him- or herself. Attempts by the group to pull the consultant into becoming a member of the group leave them further confused, and increasingly dependent on the consultant. Confusion is further added by the fact that the consultant ignores them and fails to respond to questions that members address to this non-participant. The reason consultants don't answer questions is to deter dependency and increase the learning when members themselves struggle to find answers to their questions.

It is not unusual, then, that groups tend to defend themselves against the anxiety that is a normal accompaniment of the primary task, by moving into states of mind that Bion described as basic assumption modes. At some stage, the members become anxious, not knowing where to turn to next. At this point, they are inclined to consider what they will do next. Frequently reference is made to not knowing what the task is. Possibly a member may be mobilised to read the task, but inevitably it fails to make sense, mainly because they've never before experienced a task that asks them to study their own behaviour. Thus, it is likely that another member may be mobilised to suggest a task that involves the members in an activity. Individual members of the group tend to be drawn into familiar roles through their own personal valencies.

The individual is a group animal at war, not simply with the group, but with himself or herself for being a group animal. The group brings out those valencies in which the individual is trapped and with which he has to fight to achieve his individuality. Thus, a member who has a strong dependency valency is likely to be mobilised by the group to suggest an alternative task, providing an action that will relieve the pressure on the group that is experiencing incompetence and failure regarding the task of studying the behaviour of the group, as a group, as it happens. Like all basic assumption group leaders, the leader will fail and most likely be replaced by a further basic assumption leader, who will also fail.

The consultant role

The consultant, working to task, and essentially taking up his role as consultant to the process of carrying out the various tasks, will be available to the membership, by exploring the unconscious dynamics that seem to be affecting the behaviour and the attitudes of the membership to whom they are consulting. In doing so, they use their own experience, including feelings and impulses, as source material to facilitate their understanding of the dynamics of the small study groups.

In Chapter 2, I described something of the approach that the consultant in a group relations conference might take in this setting. The most important messages, are conveyed unconsciously.

In his roles, the consultant allows this process to happen while he monitors his emotional and psychological state for signs that an unconscious connection has occurred. The consultant has first to allow an unconscious processing to occur within him so that, at some point, an idea will emerge. This is what Bion called the "selected fact". At that point the consultant will have to come to a view as to how to use this information in a way that the group can actually understand and which will further the work—that is to say, will be in the service of the task.

The task of the consultant in a group relations situation is to expose the way that the group and the individual in it are managing feelings and ideas stirred up by the very business of there being processes going on in the room that make them anxious about working together. It is the task that distinguishes the role of group consultant; it does so not only in terms of how to use information that is conveyed both consciously and unconsciously, but also in terms of how to use the self. This particularly applies to emotions and feelings. The consultant, by being in touch with his feelings, will also have the vital understanding of the feelings of the group.

An interpretation offers an understanding of material and behaviour at a deep level, not merely at a surface level. At first members will only be able to stick with the surface, obvious, meaning of their behaviour and reject the deeper level. This is a phenomenon that alters as the group develops over time. Members get the hang of unconscious meaning as it applies to others in the group remarkably quickly. It takes them longer to recognise that they, too, have an unconscious. The role of the consultant will proceed in the same way as the members', moving from simple interpretations such as, "The group is avoiding the task," to interpretations at a deeper level, such as, "The group is suffering anxiety because of their inability to work at the task and are therefore mobilising one of the members to take the group into flight." By the end of day one, most of the members will understand the way the group is using (or mobilising) members as a defence against the feelings of incompetence experienced as a result of continuing to fail to work to task.

Bion (1961) provides a powerful schema for understanding the dynamics of the group at work. The tension between the group's relatively sophisticated capacity to work at its primary task and the powerful regressive pull of the unconscious forces that Bion characterised as the basic assumptions, helps make sense of much apparently nonsensical and time-wasting behaviour in any group's functioning.

Bion recognised that being a group animal goes to the very heart of what it is to be human. He writes:

> The individual is, and always has been, a member of a group, even if his membership of it consists of behaving in such a way that reality is given to an idea that he does not belong to a group at all. The individual is a group animal at war, both with the group and with those aspects of his personality that constitute his "groupishness". ... In fact, no individual, however isolated in time or space, should be regarded as outside a group or lacking in active manifestations of group psychology. (Bion, 1961, p. 167–168)

Basic assumption groups

Each of the three basic assumption patterns (dependence, fight–flight, pairing) is characterised by a distinct emotional state. We have seen that basic assumptions are distinct from one another. Yet they also share certain qualities: they are instinctive, and no training or preparation is required to engage in them. They are oriented not towards reality, but towards internal phantasy, acting upon this impulsively and uncritically There is no need for cooperation between group members at this level of functioning: instead, individuals naturally possess what Bion described as valency—the capacity for a chemical-like attraction and spontaneous combination of one individual with another for sharing and acting on a basic assumption.

Basic assumptions start off within the individual as powerful emotions associated with a particular cluster of ideas that compel the individual to behave in a certain way and, as well, to be attracted to others imbued with the same feeling. Bion likened this to the existence of tropism in plants, in contrast to more purposive behaviour. One could say that valency in the basic assumption group corresponds to cooperation in the work group. But while cooperation requires thought, training, and maturity, valency occurs spontaneously as a function of human gregariousness. Everyone has the capacity to enter into group life, especially into the irrational and unconscious aspects of group life—though individuals will vary in the extent to which this will be so.

Bion uses the notion of schism to describe the defence against the "development of a threatening idea". This occurs when a group appears to operate along two apparently opposing lines, although actually both sides have the same end in mind—thus ensuring no development. One side sticks to a dependent unthinking position, promoting platitudes and truisms and thus avoiding thought and development. The other gives the impression of supporting development, but becomes so pedantic and exacting in its efforts that it too avoids any creative progression.

Any one of the three types of basic assumption group may underlie the work group.

The work group

I shall start from a work group situation where the group is engaged with achieving the task for which it has met. In many situations the group may find that its task is one which is perfectly within its collaborative capabilities and continues to work in that mode. The work group mobilises internal resources and relates to external realities for the performance of the task. The work group is that aspect of group functioning which has to do with the real task of the group. Whatever the formal purpose or task that the group has met to achieve, be that a planning meeting, a review meeting, or a group employed on an assembly line, the work group can define its task and is actively pursuing its achievement.

By way of example, we might consider a management team group in an organisation which meets regularly to review performance. When functioning as a work group there may be several identifiable processes that characterise such a group. The members of a work group act in a cooperative manner, each member contributing his skill and knowledge. Those present are all willing members of the group who are intent on pursuing the purpose for which they have met. They constantly review and test their progress in achieving their purpose. They are willing to learn from the experience and adopt a creative approach in achieving their purpose. And, they will be aware of the necessity to observe the constraints of time boundaries.

In reality we seldom participate in such a wonderful experience but we do often find that those meetings that we leave, congratulating ourselves and perhaps the chair or other group leader, all share many of the above characteristics. The fact that these are positive experiences should not cause us to forget that the members will still experience the group at a deep unconscious level as a maternal holding environment. In this particular situation the group provides for and encourages deeply primitive feelings associated with loving, satisfaction, and nurturing. It is a truly idealised situation where the group is credited with all the positive feelings that we associate with the good and nurturing mother.

A simple description of the work group is that it is a real or conscious process, where the group is working to task, in a collaborative way.

Valency

Valency is a term which is used to refer to the individual's readiness to enter into collaboration with the group in meeting and acting on the basic assumptions. All of us have a valency to act in one particular way more so than another. We all have a tendency to enter into group life, in particular into the irrational and unconscious aspects of group life in a particular way. Some may have a greater valency towards dependency, others towards fight–flight, and others towards pairing, and usually one of these will predominate. Individual valency will in all likelihood depend upon the early individual experiences of the maternal holding environment.

Bion's view was that such valencies are part of the biological or physiological aspect of our psyche, part of human heritage. It was their very existence, he thought, that enabled the individual to become part of a group. However, it is this same capacity that raises anxiety, because the individual becomes alarmed at the prospect of becoming merged with or submerged in the group mind—and thereby loses his own mind, or individuality. Bion felt that the idea of a primitive group unconscious that, developmentally speaking, precedes the individual's unconscious is in fact a kind of theory developed by groups themselves to account for the anxiety they are experiencing.

As well as varying in the degree of valency, people also vary in the kind of dependency towards which they are attracted. For example, some will tend more towards basic assumption dependency while others will be drawn towards fight–flight or pairing. Although an individual cannot alter his own unconscious tendency, it will become obvious to the group consultant to know towards which valency individual members incline. An effective group will unconsciously use the valency of its members to best effect. For example, where a work group is under pressure to produce results, a flight leader may be mobilised to support and encourage the work of the group. Where a work group is experiencing harsh and painful emotions, a dependency leader may be mobilised to calm and soothe the members to achieve their task. Bion describes the organisation and use of the basic assumptions by the work group in certain societies, or parts of a society. The Church, for example, is a major institution that mobilises and uses basic assumption dependency. In contrast, the Army mobilises basic assumption fight–flight, and the aristocracy, concerned as it is with breeding, that is to say, pairing with those designated as suitable, mobilises basic assumption pairing.

We have seen that basic assumptions are distinct from one another. Yet they also share certain qualities: they are instinctive, and no training or preparation is required to engage in them. They are oriented not towards reality, but towards internal phantasy, acting upon this impulsively and uncritically. There is no need for cooperation between group members at this level of functioning: instead, individuals naturally possess a valency—the capacity for a chemical-like attraction and spontaneous combination of one individual with another for sharing and acting on a basic assumption.

The group brings out those valencies in which the individual is trapped and with which he has to fight to achieve his individuality. The organisation in groups tends towards oppression. While examining this, Bion was asking the question, What is the equivalent of neurosis in the group? He wrote: "In the treatment of the individual, neurosis is displayed as a problem of the individual. In the situation of the group it must be displayed as a problem of the group" (1961, p. 11).

The mechanism responsible for this process of "becoming a member of a group" is the individual's valency, or propensity for adopting or falling into one or another of the basic assumption modes of functioning. For example:

- One individual may incline towards a dependent state of mind (ba dependency) within a group
- Another may take up a belligerent stance, another an anxious, timid position (ba fight–flight), and
- Yet another may seek for a partner or soulmate to cling to (ba pairing).

From the perspective of a group as a whole, we can understand that group members will be mobilised to be basic assumption leaders, as a means of avoiding the anxiety arising from not being able to do the task. Depending on the needs of the group, the member with the relevant valency will be unconsciously mobilised. Thus, if the group wants someone to lead it in flight, it will not mobilise a fight leader, and so on. The important question for consultants is to ask members why they are mobilising a flight leader. The aim thereby is to get the group to work beneath the surface, as opposed to making an interpretation that they are avoiding the task, which does not include a "because clause".

Thus far in this chapter we have concentrated on what happens in groups but have not explicitly explored the boundaries or constitution of groups. Yet we will be aware that even a random collection of individuals may come together to complete a task of some sort. Given the complexity of establishing what is and what is not a group, it may be helpful to view organisations from a systems perspective.

Systems

The group relations tradition developed its "knowledge base" through experience within the group relations trainings as well as from organisational consultation, in particular, through an approach that has become described as "action research" (Lewin, 1951; see pp. 21–22 for a fuller explanation of open systems theory).

Most importantly for our purposes, taking a systems perspective provides us with an opportunity to identify and make sense of some of the informal social systems that are present in our organisations. In many instances, nothing on the organisational structure charts will give an indication of this sort of system and those outside the system may not be aware of its existence. By taking a systems approach we may be able to develop the concept of a social system which may lead to a deeper understanding of the dynamics of the organisation. When we take a group-as-a-whole perspective it is important that we are able to identify these informal social systems to enable us to discover what they are representing for the organisation.

As we have seen, a group can divide in any number of ways and subgroups may form for any manner of reasons. For example, a group may divide on any one or more of the following lines: race, gender, new members and old members, and old and young, or whatever. In each instance we may view these subgroups as being mobilised to represent something or to do something on behalf of the whole group. These are all groups that are unconsciously mobilised for psychological purposes. They may be of a temporary nature or more enduring, and each individual may belong to more than one of these subgroups. Viewing groups from a systems perspective and identifying those subgroups may be a very rewarding activity.

Boundaries are relatively easily defined in biological and physical systems—they are visible. For example, we can define the physical boundaries of the human body very precisely. But how can we define the sociological and psychological boundaries of human behaviour? We must begin to define this boundary in terms of activities or processes rather than physical structures. Social systems such as organisations do not have any precise physical boundaries. Generally speaking, those activities necessary for the organisation's transformation process defines its boundary.

Some of the most important boundaries are the psychological boundaries of the groups, which define who belongs to the group and who does not. We distinguish external boundaries separating members from non-members, and internal boundaries in the context of the influence of the group on the individual. That is, we distinguish external boundaries between the "me" and the "not me" and we distinguish internal boundaries between the "in-group" and the others; or between the group and an individual or subgroup that is perhaps scapegoated or in some other way psychologically excluded.

By adopting a systems approach we can expose the way that what we are dealing with in social system transitions is fundamental change at two distinct levels at the same time: the social and the psychological. It also exposes the fact that the principles by which change takes place at each of these levels are quite different. We need to bear in mind that the environmental contexts in which organisations exist are themselves changing, at an increasing rate, and towards increasing complexity. This will increase the anxiety on those responsible for the management of organisations as they seek to develop innovative responses. In these circumstances, taking a systems approach may become even more valuable as a means of making sense of that complexity.

This is not least important because this process will expose the beneath-the-surface dynamics that managers also need to consider as part of that innovative process. To simply take the view that the formal structure is a rational and sensible process is to deny the fact that the organisational structure is intermeshed with the elements of the psychological subsystem. Simply formulating a structure with strategy and technology in mind and ignoring the psychological needs of individuals may result in anxiety and social structures as a defence against that anxiety which are anti-task.

Observing, and thinking, from a systems perspective enables a group relations consultant to gain a deeper understanding of the dynamics occurring in a group, and to make an interpretation that provides the members with learning at a beneath-the-surface level.

CHAPTER 4

The large study group (LSG)

Large study group

The large group is defined simply as one in which face-to-face relation-ships are no longer possible. It is comprised of individuals and of small groups, who may or may not be organised informally. The members of a large group will also be grouped informally in static changing patterns. The internal life of the large group consists therefore of the relationships between individuals, and of the relationships within and between the small groups to which they belong. Individuals have their own needs and unconscious motives, and the small groups, their tasks and basic assumptions. Without a formal structure to define its task, its bound-aries, and its role system, the large group is thus the victim of con-fused individual strivings and small-group assumptions. If the same basic assumption prevails simultaneously in all small study groups that compose the large group, the attitudes and feelings associated with the assumption are powerfully reinforced. In such circumstances appeals to reason, to thought before action, have little chance of success. The group moves impulsively and with compelling force. If different basic assumptions prevail in different parts of the large group, small group membership can change with bewildering rapidity as individuals try to join up with those in unconscious collusion with themselves. The resulting pattern is one of confusion, inaction, futility, and frustration. In this condition, an individual who can define some positive goal can exercise powerful leadership.

As with the small study group, the task of the large study group (LSG) is also to provide opportunities to learn about interpersonal relations as they happen, but in a setting in which the number of members is larger than can form a face-to-face group. Again, the task is to study the behaviour of the group, as a group, as it happens. However, in this group, the individual may not only face the other individuals, they may also face major subgroups, in the form of study groups or spontaneously created subgroups. Members may seek anonymity in a subgroup or as a member of the whole.

Large groups, those too big for every member to know every other by face and name, differ considerably from small study groups. Many of an individual's capacities for reflection, thought, problem-solving, and decision-making—important elements of his identity—may be overwhelmed and subsumed by the large group itself. Both followers and followed are at risk from the kinds of projective and introjective processes engendered by large groups.

Even in the small group, it is not easy to expose one's feelings or to put forward ideas that have not been fully formulated, but at least the attempt can be made in an atmosphere of intimacy. In the small group, as compared with the large group, the individual is more likely to have a chance to explain him- or herself without being made to feel guilty about taking more than a fair share of the available time, and to speak without feeling that he will be irrevocably committed to a point of view and have little or no opportunity of correcting him- or herself. The large group provides a more public occasion, and the greater the number present, the greater the exposure. The large group, therefore, poses special problems for its members and leaders. It demands different qualities of its leaders and different kinds of communication between its members if task performance is to be effective.

The small group is one in which each member is known to the others in the group and each can give a personal account of the other. This is certainly not true of large groups, where many a member remains an unknown quantity throughout. Not being face to face, not being encompassable at a glance by any one member, the kind of personal interaction with other members and with the whole, which is characteristic of the individual's experience in small groups, is no longer possible. The individual may suffer a sense of dislocation as they go from a small to a large group.

There is usually space outside the seating provided, permitting each member in the outside seating to move, as he wishes, either towards or away from the centre of the spiral. Such a structure undoubtedly contributes to the member's experience of being in space, surrounded by other members. This heightens inter-membership experience and seems to influence and give significance to a member's choice of seat. As a result, each of the seating positions acquires its own characteristic feeling tone, with a varying range of experiences for each member, depending on the location in which they are seated, and with, correspondingly, a varying sense of being in or out, marginally or centrally committed to participation, the object of the group's pressures, or left in peace.

A measure of the discomfort experienced by members of a large group is the fact that, apart from a few scattered subgroups that may hang around, I cannot recall any occasion when a large group chose to continue beyond the time boundary, as sometimes happens with the small groups. Thus, while problems of commitment are prominent, the wish to get out is even more important. However, I am describing the initial stages of large-group life, the first session of its existence, where a member's anxiety might be expected to be at its height, and where unfamiliarity, both with the overall situation and with the other members, is maximal.

The large-group exercise may often feature challenges to the structure. Often the membership will not know that the staff have already debated, very seriously, how to set up the room. My own preference, when working on a group relations conference, is for the "spiral" seating system. Equally, the task, to study the behaviour of the group, as a group, as it happens, will have been thought about carefully and then written down and read out by either the director or by the consultant responsible for the large group. Nevertheless, the conference members will find reasons to complain about seating, about "the attitude" of the staff group (as yet unknown), the lack of direction, or the environment itself.

The membership will comprise the whole conference membership and the staff; from thirty to sixty in total. The spiral seating is important, and is the closest we can get to producing the experience of being in a large group. Here, it's only possible to talk to the people each side of you, and you only see the backs of people immediately in front of you. Thus, the large-group experience cannot be encompassed by any one of its members in a single glance. Each single member is surrounded on all sides, in front, behind, to the left and to the right, except those in the back row, who have nobody behind them. This, in itself, is a big surprise for the members as they enter the large-group room.

As stated above, the task is that which applies to all conference events. The study is self-study, in which the consultant's interpretations play their part. The overall context of these conferences, as also of each event within them, is experiential—a self-acquisition of insight from experienced happenings—and is therefore not directly didactic. The model is basically that of Freudian psychoanalysis, with a deliberate and conscious attempt to refrain from any form of telling (or teaching). Thus, events are fundamentally allowed to take their own course. The consultants do not propose a subject for discussion, usually remaining silent at the beginning of a session, unless able to make some immediate comment on an aspect of the actual opening: for example, major chair rearrangements, lateness, and the like. Their task is to take up topics and behaviour as they emerge. Like all free-associative situations, the topics, and behaviours are viewed as being determined by the under-lying dynamic interaction in which both the group and its members, including the consultants, find themselves.

The basic notion, then, is the presence of a dynamic interaction between large group and members, an interaction in which all events, whether nonverbal or spoken, are an expression of a process which is there to be understood. Clearly, the task of understanding is a difficult one; nor are the consultants working solely with forces directed at self-understanding, though self-understanding is an essential part of the large group's primary task and reason for existence.

Threats to identity in the large group

Because the group is perceived at a deeply unconscious level as a mater-nal entity, we might not think it unusual if the conflicted nature of a conference would lead to anxiety and that this evokes in the individual primordial struggles similar to those experienced as a child. These may include wishes for fusion and merger as against separateness and loneliness; powerful experiences of satisfaction, nurturing, and frustration; acute ambivalence—emotional (love–hate) and defensive (splitting and projective identification); and tensions between engulfment and estrangement.

The group as a whole is likely to be viewed by the individual member as an instrument for conscious need satisfaction. This will include a broad range of needs that includes those of an educational or ideological nature. Group associations are also sought to gratify less articulated needs such as those for belonging, for emotional support, for protection, and for self-help. At the deeper regressive level, the group holding environment can be perceived by the individual as the symbolic representation of a nurturing mother.

However, the group situation can raise feelings of ambivalence and anxiety. The elements of this discomfort may be traced back to earliest infancy where the infant experiences two opposing sets of feelings and impulses, libidinal and aggressive. These stem from instinctual sources and are described by the constructs of the life instinct and the death instinct. The infant feels omnipotent and attributes dynamic reality to these feelings and impulses. He believes that the libidinal impulses are literally life-giving and the aggressive impulses death-dealing. At this early stage of life, the infant is still part of a dyad and has not yet developed the concept of individuation. The infant attributes similar feelings, impulses, and powers to other people and to important parts of people. The objects and the instruments of the libidinal and aggressive impulses are felt to be the infant's own and other people's bodies and bodily products. Physical and psychic experiences are very intimately interwoven at this time. The infant's psychic experience of objective reality is greatly influenced by his own feelings and phantasies, moods, and wishes.

Through this psychic experience the infant builds up an inner world peopled by himself or herself and the objects of his feelings and impulses. In this inner world they exist in a form and condition largely determined by his phantasies. Because of the operation of aggressive forces, the inner world contains many damaged, injured, or dead objects. The atmosphere is charged with death and destruction which gives rise to great anxiety. The infant, when faced with such circumstances, uses the mother to reinforce individual mechanisms of defence against anxiety, and in particular against recurrence of the early paranoid and depressive anxieties. This may seem unconnected to group and organisational processes but, as has already been discussed, the group holding environment is experienced at a deep unconscious level as a maternal entity which means we can anticipate that members of groups will experience the same sort of primordial struggles as those experienced by the infant.

The mother–infant social relationships serve a number of purposes including the important expression and gratification of libidinal impulses in constructive social activities, as well as social cooperation in organisations and institutions providing creative, sublimatory opportunities. Many of these beneath-the-surface processes will tend to encourage a positive task-supporting culture. However, here in this subsection we are primarily concerned with the effects of a defensive function. As we as members of groups or organisations treat the group or organisational holding environment as if it were the maternal holding environment, we should perhaps not be surprised that in much the same way as in the infant–mother relationship, organisations and institutions are used by their individual members to fill the same needs. When we suffer anxiety, we use the group in the mind to reinforce our mechanisms of defence.

One of the primary cohesive elements binding individuals into institutionalised human association is that of defence against psychotic anxiety. In this sense, individuals may be thought of as externalising those impulses and internal objects that would otherwise give rise to psychotic anxiety, and pooling them in the life of the social institutions in which they associate. This does not mean that the institutions become "psychotic". But it does imply that we would expect to find in group relationships manifestations of unreality, splitting, hostility, suspicion, and other forms of maladaptive behaviour. These would be the social counterpart of—although not identical with—what would appear as psychotic symptoms in individuals who have not developed the ability to use the mechanism of association in social groups to avoid psychotic anxiety.

There are powerful forces at work, no respecters of persons, seeking to change the role and status of every individual member of the large group. The struggle to resist them, to remain an individual, is great.

In the harsh terms of large-group life, it is a case of who will dominate whom. Only withdrawal can lessen the struggle for the individual. Participation and self-exposure are the only way to survive.

Inevitably in a situation so constantly suffused with the struggle to dominate, survival—if it is to be at a creative level—will have idiosyncratic aspects. The major large-group defence against such forces is by homogenisation, that is, survival by all being alike, sinking or swimming together. But homogenisation is a pure survival mechanism: its creative powers are nil. To be creative in the large group requires standing to be counted, which implies from the point of view of other members idiosyncrasy of self-expression or self-assertion. It is clear from this that the approach from the point of view of the individual member experiencing aspects of this conversion process is not a sociological one, though hopefully, the sociological implications of the individual member's dilemmas and experiences may emerge.

Given the stressful and traumatic experiences of the large group, we should not be surprised that the group responds by freezing.

The modern human brain reflects millions of years of evolutionary adaptation that is driven and directed by the physical survival functioning based on primitive fight or flight mechanisms of the species, not by the happiness of individuals. Thus, much of the brain's functioning is based upon primitive fight or flight mechanisms as opposed to conscious decision-making. Fear and anxiety remain the core components of our attachment relationships.

How does evolution make its choices? An important example can be seen in the conservation of the primitive deer-in-the-headlights startle response. Think about a time when you were startled: did you come to an abrupt stop, freeze all your movements and hold your breath as you try responses to maximise the ability to avoid detection, locate the source of possible danger, and prepare to fight or flee? As sophisticated as language has become, it is still the creation of sound that might expose us to danger. Because of this, the freeze response results in the inhibition of language in highly stressful and traumatic situations.

Fight and flight are the basic responses of all animals to situations that evoke pain or the threat of danger. There is a further such response that Bion does not refer to, that of freezing, which I refer to as "ba freezing". We see this in individuals in situations that evoke the threat of danger, for example when an individual is threatened with a weapon or the prospect of rape. The individual first assesses whether to fight or flee but when that seems impossible, they may freeze. The same thing is evoked in groups where the group as a whole acts in a similar manner as "ba freezing".

Inevitably the lack of structure, and, as to topic, freedom to contribute as and when a member wishes, and the offered absence of restraints on individual behaviour, contribute to the general strangeness and unexpectedness of the situation. It reflects the general conference philosophy of wishing to study what emerges, and to give the joining member as he arrives at the conference the freedom to examine the conference events in his own particular way. Both tasks—to explore conference events and to do so as one wishes—have their difficulties, their development being a further object for study.

The aim of the conferences is equally important and is designed to be educational and not therapeutic. Members come for study and learning, not as patients; any therapeutic gain is a chance, though acceptable, by-product. It is true that the overall tone of the meetings is experiential and teaching in the accepted sense is only occasionally provided, but the aim is through interpretations to help the membership to come to grips with its own behaviour in the "here and now" and hence be insightful about it and possibly change it. In this sense too, the large group is unstructured since no learning targets are set. Each member is free to experience and determine his own learning within his relationship both to the total situation and to the consultants.

The member who, though he wishes to participate in the group's activities, and through participation to study the behaviour of a large group, should at this entry stage be thought of as a singleton. Here at once is one of the major problems in describing large-group experiences: what terms are to be used to describe the changing states of its members? Turquet (1974) introduced the term "singleton" for this person entering into a new experience totally on his own, not yet part of a group but attempting both to find himself or herself and to make relations with the other singletons who are in a similar state.

One of the characteristics of a large group is that many of its members remain in the singleton state, unable, possibly unwilling, to join in and so to go through a necessary change of state. This conversion process is part of the dislocation every conference member experiences as he takes himself or herself into a world which transcends the usual parameters of their own individuality. Turquet also found it necessary to have a term for the singleton who has established a relationship, not only with the large group as a whole, but also with the other singletons, each and all having thereby evolved out of their singleton states. Such converted singletons he referred to as individual members.

Turquet also developed the notion of one more important state to be identified: a transitional one, as the individual member in their group life moves between the various states of singleton to individual member and back to singleton. The notion of a conversion process adds weight and value to such interim states, however transitory. Theoretically at least, they represent choice of opportunities, the choice of the member to be this or that, an individual member or to revert to a singleton state, or to opt out. The exercise of such choice, whether consciously known or not, is the occasion for the expression of individuality.

Assuming, therefore, that there is a struggle within the individual to resist the conversion process in the group, these transitional states may allow him, whatever group membership role he may have been in, to reassert his own particular individuality, possibly in a sudden upsurge of idiosyncratic behaviour. It seems reasonable to refer to the member involved in this transitional moment as an "I" and to call that sudden upsurge of "himselfness" or "herselfness" a state of "I-ness". Clearly, both terms reflect once again the struggle between singleton and large group, with the singleton wishing to interact with the large group and thereby to find an individual member role for himself or herself.

The I's need for a boundary or skin is the critical difficulty for the singleton on entering a large group, and finding himself or herself in this strange and unfamiliar situation the first challenge is to find a point of entry: how to start an interactional relationship between himself or herself and its members, as also with the total situation. The experience is essentially one of search, the search for some tool, idea, concept, with which to come to grips with the experiences he is having and by entering the interactive process to move from being a singleton to become a "joiner"—an I interacting at the interface—and so to establish himself or herself as an individual member.

The sense of threat of becoming other than himself or herself, of being in some way altered, pressurised, even diminished, is for the singleton an ever-present experience as he lives in the large group.

It is remorseless, to be constantly guarded against, that is, if a member wishes to maintain individual member status. Without this external boundary, puppetry is a constant possibility, to be fended off by withdrawal. So important is the "skin-of-my-neighbour" (i.e. a sense of connection with an other who is close but also separate (Turquet, 1975)) for the singleton in a large group that he will seek to go into a large-group session flanked on either side, that is, as a threesome. In small groups, by contrast, a member is more easily content with paired relationships. If the individual member status is not securely established, the various problematical processes have foiled him and the defensive manoeuvres have broken down. From such a background the interacting singleton can say, "This is me now—that was me then." The presence of the past as part of a background boundary skin enables the singleton to live and interact in the "here-and-now" happenings of the large group, that is, whatever may be emerging or occurring in the large group at any one moment in the present time. This background boundary skin has a further important special aspect. While the presence of the past gives rise to a sense of continuity of growth out of all our yesterdays, the singleton's immediate experience is nevertheless one of discontinuity, of being different, of being other than he was yesterday, to the extent of his saying: "I am no longer like that," or even "I don't want to be like that."

The interdependence of these two boundary aspects in a singleton's "here-and-now" experiential life should be stressed. Thus, while the presence of the other as an individual member inherently carries an element of separation and detachment, and even of a forceful pulling away ("That is not me," or more crudely: "That's what you think; I think differently"), the background of time past equally inherently carries a desire to fuse the certainty of yesterday's there and then, the uncertainty of today's "here and now", and the unknown-ness of tomorrow. On the one hand, the singleton's experience of present living, with the past its own discrete content of repeated separations from the past, by its very discontinuities may come to reinforce a wish to maintain contact with the "other", who by his presence seems to offer some experiential assurance of continuous existence in the "here and now" and hence of survival from a past. Thus, the presence of the other member may stimulate the desire to fuse. On the other hand, forceful separations from the other individual members (henceforth referred to as IM), or difficulties in relating to another IM, may encourage fusion wishes with the past, which then appears as an attractive proposition—hence the "Peter Pan" wishes in us all.

Fusion and separation is thus an ever-present dynamic, the former leading on to IM and the latter leading back to a singleton state. Other factors play their part in the singleton's urge to fuse with a background, not least the sense of familiarity that the past offers. For the past seems to imply a security and an experience of events that have been lived through and from which there has been survival. Yet this past—the "what we did yesterday" discussion—is frequently non-adaptive in the face of what is happening to the struggling IM in the large group "here and now". If, as so often happens, the IM cannot recall what he did or what was happening to him yesterday, not only does the past not seem to rescue him and make him feel secure, but it now becomes a threat. What has happened to it? Vanished, like the snows of yesteryear, with a "who am I now?" feeling. Anxiety surges up with a developing content of annihilation, becoming fear of a void in which to be lost. Since internally nothing can be found, there is nothing there. The move to try to re-establish a "here-and-now" contact with the skin-of-my-neighbour can then be very quick.

The singleton's dilemma may be put very aptly: a historical sense is essential, which means that we must know how to be new as contrasted with repetition, on the one hand, and with escape from tradition, on the other. We must sit in the seats of our ancestors: we must turn our ancestors out of them. As far as man in a group is concerned, whether it be large or small, that is easier said than done. While, for the singleton, the first of these two boundary aspects, the skin-of-my-neighbour, involves the play of centrifugal forces, lest loss of self in the other members take place, with the second, the establishment of a past, its creation brings into play centripetal forces, the sense of attraction of the past away from the difficulties of present-day living. True, in both instances, it is a question of an equilibrium between the forces, with the I discovering the extent of his freedom to move in either direction.

There is much about the large group to interfere with the individual's (I's) freedom of movement. Almost immediately on entering the large group, the singleton experiences the competing presence of two forces, in terms of whether to belong or whether to pull out. Although this conflict may be true of all relationships, in the large group the polarity as experienced by the interacting but struggling singleton is, in extreme terms, either isolated apartness or a complete fusion with or loss in it. The large group reveals the singleton's difficulty in preserving an interactive psychological distance between himself or herself and the "other", be the "other" an event, an experience, or a member.

The seating in the spiral has a considerable impact on the members. Those in the middle are likely to be the subject of projections, and expected to provide leadership for the behaviour of the group, whereas those on the outer seating tend to be silent and acting more as observers. It is not unusual for those in the centre to agree to change seats with a member on the outside. It is also likely that a member sitting anywhere will withdraw from the group. This may at times be viewed as collusive behaviour by these two subgroups: the outside taking the role of holding the individualism of the group, and those in the middle providing leadership in the interests of the group.

Consultancy

The role of consultant is concerned with understanding what is going on "below the surface". Although there is tremendous pressure within the staff of a group relations conference to engage in an exploration of the pathology (deriving from the valencies) of the individual members, this is not the task. Instead, the task is to show how the anxiety consequent on being a member of a large group is creating ideas and beliefs at an unconscious level that are being treated as facts and around which individuals find themselves taking up positions.

Usually, two or more consultants are provided to help the members in their task, their numbers being related to the size of the membership and staff availability. The consultant's primary task is to interpret events, not merely describing the group behaviour, but attempting to analyse the dynamic underlying it, that is, its motivation and purpose, in terms of a "because clause". Clearly, for the consultants all kinds of problems abound, not least how they are able to function and what happens to their interpretative role. All large-group consultants are experienced individuals who from extended periods of working as consultants to small study groups, by participating in large groups, and through CPD learning, are capable of taking up a role as a large-group consultant. All have the same authority, and it is important to understand that these consultants have a dual role: that of managing the conference and of consultant.

When an individual suffers a traumatic event, he is flooded with unmanageable quantities of raw chaotic unprocessable "stuff", and his mental functioning is thrown into disarray. For a while, he is overwhelmed and out of action. When a collection of people all feel themselves to be traumatised by a particular event, each will respond in his own particular way, but there will also be much experience in common. Can one use an understanding of what happens to the individual, and the ways he begins, with or without help, to recover some sort of working equilibrium, when the group itself, and not only the individual, needs help? Or does one need to start thinking differently?

On the occasions where a single member may be projected into and is clearly overwhelmed by the experience, one or more of the consultants may judge it necessary to step in and exercise their management authority to direct the membership to "take back their projections". Where a person is projected into, they are not ill, they are simply overwhelmed by the fact that the group as a whole has projected thoughts and feelings they find unbearable into this single member. These may be feelings of incompetence, helplessness, worthlessness, any sort of negative feelings that are felt to be unbearable. The only way to relieve the individual suffering from these projections is to get the group to take back their projections. Once they do this, the single member will almost immediately recover to normality.

The presence of more than one consultant is deliberately planned to facilitate inter-consultant processes, to work together to help the members to make sense of the experiences occurring in the large group at any particular time. Consulting to a large group is a difficult task, and at any given moment several different dynamics may be occurring. Thus, it may be the case that different interpretations are given by different consultants. Here, it's important that all staff are highly competent as the members are likely to see this difference as an opportunity to create splitting of the consultants. A lone consultant could become isolated and be deskilled, filled up, threatened with annihilation—to mention but a few of the many common personal experiences provided by the large group. This is another reason why consultants work as a team. To have a role in itself increases the chances of survival, to survive being an important emergent aim in such a group. The designation of consultant gives a special and favoured position to come to grips with the behaviour of the large group and demonstrate expertise. The study of the fate of this expertise, the fluctuations in facility, the fluidity or hesitancy with which it is experienced, is not the whole of the consultant's task, but is a vital indicator of the nature of the forces acting on the consultancy role.

The consultancy team

Once the small study groups have been completed, the director will chair a staff meeting to prepare for the large study group the following day. He will start by introducing and explaining the role of the three large-group consultants, who all will be experienced consultants, with the required skills, knowledge, and ability to take up the role. He will ensure that these staff members understand that they must take up their seats in strategic positions before the members start taking their seats. It is important that consultants are able to see each other, so they can work cooperatively; and so that between them, they can view the whole membership. He will then discuss who of the staff will be selected to mark the time boundaries in each session. The staff member in the first session will also tell the members the task once he has sat down. This member may assist the administrator to usher the members in on time, he will then enter the large study group room at the stated time, to mark the time boundary, and take whatever chair that may be available. If there is a choice, he needs to take a strategic position away from the large study group consultants.

The director will then address the remaining consultants and training consultants and explain that their role is that of learning about large-group dynamics and the consultant role. Other than exceptional circumstances they should not be making interpretations.

Finally, he will inform the staff that they should not "piggy back", that is, once one consultant has made an interpretation, no other consultant should speak until at least one member has spoken.

At the conclusion of the meeting, the staff will go to the large study group room and set up the chairs in a spiral ready for the next day.

The staff will then have a short meeting the next morning in preparation for the large-group exercise.

The three large-study-group consultants will then take their places in the spiral.

At the stated time, the consultant who has opened the session will get up and end the session by walking out. If possible, he will nod their intentions to the large-study-group consultants, just prior to the time boundary.

After each session, there will be a staff meeting where the consultants will try to make sense of what is happening in the large group and work out what understanding may be helpful for the consultants to interpret for the members in the next session.

After each session, there is a need to reconfigure the spiral, to remove clothing from chairs, and to remove cups and glasses, so that the room is set for the next session.

Consultants working as a team

The conference I shall describe took place a few years ago. It began with several members becoming very oppressed by the seating arrangement in the large group. This seemed to be something to do with discomfort, particularly about not being able to be seen or not seeing. A fight leader had been mobilised to encourage the members to break the spiral and sit in a large circle whereby all could sit in comfort and see each other. A group of about ten started to move their chairs. I made an interpretation saying that this was "an attack on the learning". The staff had deliberately set up the room in this way to provide the opportunity for learning in a large group. By breaking the seating, it was an attack on the learning. The group was split between the group who had moved their chairs and a slightly larger group who expressed their wanting to learn.

Comfort is frequently a theme in the large group. However, in this instance, it was clear that there was present something much more threatening than this rather obvious difference. It is often difficult to see the issues that underlie the behaviour of the large group because such groups have a relatively limited range of expression. There is inevitably a preoccupation with the sense of being controlled by the consulting staff. Within the membership, there is always a search for a means of taking control. In this environment, individuals are provided with the opportunity to discover how easily they fall into a particular role that fosters a flight from reality. The pressure of size tends to reveal the most psychotic level of functioning in the deepest parts of the group unconscious. In the situation described above, the situation remained in being for almost an hour, after which the consultants, working as a team, brought about a return to the spiral.

In a further experience, a narcissistic member was mobilised as an alternative consultant promising to lead the group in a comfortable, enjoyable experience as opposed to the painful experience created by the consultants. Again, this seemingly helpful intervention was nothing less than an attack on the learning. However, the notion of comfort and pleasure was a very attractive proposition for members who were struggling to make sense of their difficult, and at times, painful experiences of being members of the large group. It was, then, difficult for the consultants to displace this alternative consultant. It was only finally achieved by the large-group consultants working together in a determined and professional manner.

These are both examples of forms of violence which is a significant aspect of large groups.

Violence

By virtue of the nature of the large study group with no structure or organisation, it is near inevitable that their behaviour is unpredictable. It is not unusual for the group to act as a mob, a dangerous and unruly group in the grip of a wish to locate and destroy an enemy, whether real or imagined. Those who make up a mob will stream past the voice of reality or reason. A mob hates thought. The primitive impulses that exist as a potential in every member, in every human being, can be tapped into and amplified by disturbed and unscrupulous leaders, and the outcome can be mayhem.

The phenomenon of violence, which is perhaps one of the major characteristics of the large group, especially in terms of the initial anxiety experienced by its members, is disturbing. For the control of violence, the large group has had to evolve a quite specific and characteristic structure. The idea of violence is present in many forms, often—especially initially—as a nameless fear, a threat of something that is around, something that is going to happen, voiced in such simple statements as "I am frightened". Again, it may be expressed through the I's silence, the expression of an unwillingness to talk about this fear and so give it content, as also in the quiet, lowered, almost inaudible tones adopted by some members. To talk loudly would be to lower the threshold for violence and so almost to provoke it. On talking, a member may report a sense of "being dehumanised", being made into something animal. Violence may also find expression as a fantasy directing behaviour: so that search parties are sent for absentees. No piece of behaviour can be treated as innocent, as if all behaviour was both the expression and the result of some present destructive force. The fantasy may be of something going on in the middle, as at a bullfight: the centre circle is therefore to be avoided; and of those in the outer circle as present at an entertainment occasion, expressed in almost gleeful wishes that something will happen.

The demand for action—itself a characteristic release phenomenon in groups—adds a further impetus, such action to be concrete. This search for a spectacle theme may refer to attempts to split the consultants, with the hope that they will quarrel, contradict each other, or otherwise get at each other's throats. Hence the need for highly competent group relations consultants. Violence in its chief expression, however, is a myth, being the product of inter-member interactions in group situations: the myth of mob rule, or the myth of errant forces at work, as in the immediate object of the violence in some IM, usually one who is seeking to maintain and develop his individuality. Such behaviour or expression of personal feeling, and then of this silence, which is the upsurge of I-ness, is totally unacceptable. Its implied individuality is anathema, it must be crushed. Thus an IM remarks, "I nearly burst into tears," and his statement is greeted with laughter. He is left isolated, almost a figure of fun.

Another, who has been a note-taker and has made it quite clear that for him note-taking is a vital means of surviving, reports that he has not been able to continue doing so, and the response is again loud, massive, and at times manic laughter. He was on the road to being thrown; his defence was personal; the laughter now completely throws him and nobody protests. An IM thinks that he has learned something from the large group and is challenged to explain what it is. He tries to do so, fumblingly tails off, and the group's response is mocking laughter, never help. Or, as a member also tries to express something personal as an IM, some feeling that he has had about the large group, the tension will noticeably rise as he is questioned and in turn, strives to explore and explain himself or herself. Hopefully, it seems that he may fail; there is relief if he gets through. Often it will be some volunteer who is egged on: "Why don't you try? Go on, do it," or: "You say you are frightened, why don't you leave?" At the same time, he is filled up with other IM statements and there is no let-up: "You say you are upset. Why don't you tell us some more?" Once the process is on, there is no crying off or stopping. In such circumstances the IM feels threatened in his role: the I-state emerges, with the search to express some personal, intimate part of himself—his I-ness—or herself—her I-ness, and the large group, by this "say more" behaviour, seems to encourage this very self-expression. At such a moment as this, transitional I is at his most vulnerable. To him, it appears that the large group wishes to be present at his annihilation. It seems that the wish is to take into an IM, his role and state to be solely defined by the group: "Tell us—go on—explain more—What do you mean?", so to become the object of this large group's will.

It should be noted that although on such occasions some members do go along with such "hunt" situations, they remain silent and seem unable to exercise any authority over it. Nor does their silence help the endangered I. The I may thereby take the drastic step of withdrawing—though he is not in too good a condition to achieve this if the imagined breakdown (fantasied too as the group's aim and maybe with some reality) is not to occur. Under such conditions, breakdowns are not unknown. It is then that disarray threatens and alienation can occur. A further aggravation may arise from the IM's wish, or his seeming wish, in the eyes of other IMs, to support the work of the consultants. By so doing, he may be judged to be thinking for himself or herself, which in itself is heinous. To work with the consultants not only helps to make the IM state more secure, it also certainly helps in the struggle not to become an IM. But with the emergence of violence, the large group and its members are projectively identified with this aim that seeks to put its mark on all the members.

Hence the vulnerability of the fumbling transitional I at such moments. The I's crucial struggle is to seek to re-establish his IM role and hence survive. To do so is to escape the large group's imprint. Only if he becomes an IM will the large group be satisfied. Participation in large groups is thus fraught with dangerous ambiguities: who to be? what will happen?—ambiguities which, as the scent is to the hunt, add their quota of danger and hence of violence.

The size of the large group is frightening: violence then, is the outcome of the fears and frustrations of expressing oneself in such a large-group situation. Part of the fear is: what will the vast size of the large group do to the small individual singleton or IM? The difficulties in finding roles and the constant threat of loss of skills do not help the IM to have confidence in the potential benevolence of the large group or the hope of acquiring a stature adequate to its mastery. The fragmentation of the I, both through response bombardment and through multiple projections, serves to weaken his search for IM status, and hence he becomes vulnerable. The frequent and repeated rupture of the IM's preferred social response distance means that his boundary at his neighbour's skin is in constant flux. Nor is his vulnerability reduced by his frequent periods of abstraction as he breaks off contact from the immediacy of the large group to take stock of his situation, and thereby ruptures his contact with his neighbour's skin.

It is an impoverished IM who is trying to deal with this situation, whose efforts are directed at keeping his skin intact as best he can though in a puny way. It is very difficult, if not almost impossible, for an IM to develop the skills requisite for the maintenance of that role in the absence of an experience of successful work. Thus, the flux of the I state is on him. Whichever way he turns, disarray and alienation threaten. Overall, it is as if the I, as he strives to remain in continuous contact with the rapidly deteriorating there-and-now situation of the large group and seeks to establish and maintain the IM role, becomes the very seat of an atomic explosion with a consequent release of enormous destructive forces, directed against all that the situation contains. Violence emerges. Coming from more than one IM, it summates. The problem of violence, especially in its origin, interacts with the question of the location of responsibility.

The consultants and violence

Much of this violence, especially in the early stages of its emergence, is experienced by the consultants as well as directed at them. They will be told not to exaggerate as if, echo-wise, this would bring the felt violence into being. It is stressed that they should be ultra-professional and neutral, all anger, sarcasm, rebukes—these being members' fantasies about their tone of voice—to be kept at bay as if they might give expression to such feelings by their behaviour and reflect the anger that is around, hastening the onset of violence. They are heard as voicing the unmentionable.

Furthermore, like the members, the consultants experience the strength of the deskilling that takes place in these circumstances and which threatens their capacity for effective work. As already mentioned, consultants experience difficulty in working at a description of the situation and at their interpretations. It is borne in on them that there will be pleasure if they fail and that they are struggling with forces which seek to prevent their finding the necessary concepts and holding ideas. They are to be homogenised like the rest. They too therefore experience personal needs for self-assertion. To start talking may be a means whereby a consultant recovers his memory. But as he works to put internal distance between his actual experience and his working self, he can never be sure that he will come across his explanation of the underlying dynamic. That too may have disappeared in the welter of internalised cross-talk. It is hard work—touch and go. It would seem then that a consultant's difficulties mirror the members' difficulties.

Often these difficulties result in his making more frequent interventions than he might in other situations, for instance in a small group.

Technically this may be wise; for increased frequency of interventions has in itself a stabilising and normative effect, though it may encourage the use of the consultants as a projection receptacle. In this context of violence, the notion of the consultants acting as a projection receptacle, especially if there are three or four of them, is very important. It is certainly a dynamic to which they must be sensitive. Each consultant must therefore give an important part of his attention to its study, and seek to include in it not only what is being put into him individually but what is also being put into his colleagues, how they are being used relationally, individually, and as a subgroup, and hence to elucidate the nature of the overall picture that between them they have come to represent. What the consultants experience in this situation becomes more and more a mirror image of the experience and fate of each individual member, and hence may have important foretelling aspects, particularly with regard to the possible presence of violent destructive forces.

Because very often the anger of the IM or of the I caught in such processes is a projected anger, the recipient being the consultant, and because it rarely comes from one source but from many and hence has a summation quality to it, this anger in transit may be experienced as arising quite suddenly within the introjecting consultant. Additionally, he may be the only consultant to experience it, because as part of a more general splitting process the other consultants are to be split off from him. As part of his work, however, he will start to talk about the experience of being angry, thereby using it constructively. He may then counter a not unusual response from the IM's frank disbelief. This disbelief may have two further consequences. First, to talk, leave him with the anger and hence to isolate him. Second, to fill him up further with angry reproaches: "How can he say such a thing?", "It must be his imagination!", or "I get really pissed off when I hear the consultants talk like that"—which serves to isolate him further. Now his survival is at stake. To climb back, as it were, or get on top of this situation, he may have to use force, maybe by speaking loudly or emphatically, commanding silence by his weighty entry or personal self-assertiveness: so, to be told he is obviously angry. Something of an impasse is reached. To be silent about such experiences originating from the group is to go under. To assert such experiences verbally is to be violent. The technical solution is the interpretation of both aspects—to go under or to survive by domination—where both aspects reflect also the IM's problems, when he is at risk as an I. This situation of violence comes about from a number of factors, each reinforcing the other.

Work group and basic assumptions

In the work group individuals remain individuals and cooperate, whereas in the basic assumption group they are swept spontaneously by the "valency" of identification, the primitive gregarious quality in the personality, into the undifferentiated unity of the ba group in which inner realities overwhelm the relationship with the real task.

In his review of the dynamics of the group Bion hopes to show that:

> in his contact with the complexities of life in a group the adult resorts, in what may be a massive regression, to mechanisms described by Melanie Klein (1931, 1946) as typical as the earliest phases of mental life. The adult must establish contact with the emotional life of the group in which he lives; this task would appear to be as formidable to the adult as the relationship with the breast appears to be to the infant, and the failure to meet the demands of this task is revealed in his regression. (1961, p. 139)

The two main features of this regression are, first, a belief that the group exists as an entity which is endowed with characteristics by each individual. Distinct individuals become lost and the group is treated as if it were another person. Second is the change within the individual that accompanies his regressed perception of the group. For this change, Bion quotes Freud's description of the loss of the individual's distinctiveness, with the addition that the individual's struggle to retain it varies with the state of the group. Organisation helps to maintain work-group activity, and indeed that is its aim.

The individual loses his effectiveness when in a basic assumption group, that is, one in which individuality is swamped by the group valencies. When it has to deal with realities, such a group has to change or perish. Members can recognise themselves as torn between the pull of the basic groups and membership of the work group which represents ego functioning. What he asserts is that by showing the group the ways it avoids its task through dependency, fight–flight, or pairing, it can become more work oriented and so further the development by learning of all members.

As might be expected given the difficult environment of the large study group, there will be considerable use of basic assumption behaviours. What is likely to be impossible is the notion of a work group. Indeed, one of the essential learnings from the experience of working in a large group is that this is not something that should be contemplated in organisations of every kind. The only valid purpose for using large groups in organisations is to communicate information to large numbers at the same time.

In addition to basic assumption behaviours, we can identify two other frequently used processes, namely, projective identification and social systems as a defence against anxiety.

Social systems as a defence against anxiety

One of the ways that members of groups, organisations, and institutions deal with their anxiety is to develop social structures as a defence against perceived anxiety. These will then appear as elements in the organisation's structure, culture, and mode of functioning (see p. 22 and pp. 123–127 for more on this).

The characteristic feature of the social defence system is its orientation to helping the individual avoid the experience of anxiety, guilt, doubt, and uncertainty. Defences are, and can only be, operated by individuals but these are part of group dynamics arising from the notion of the group as a whole. A social defence system develops over time as the result of collusive interaction and agreement, often unconscious, between members of the group as to what form it shall take. An important aspect of such socially structured defence mechanisms is that they are an attempt by individuals to externalise and give substance on objective reality to their characteristic psychic defence mechanisms. This may be achieved by splitting and projective identification. The socially structured defence mechanisms then tend to become an aspect of external reality.

In so far as feelings cannot be worked with personally, they are likely to be dealt with by the development of defences against them, and will come to be built into the structure, culture, and mode of functioning of the large group and thereby impair performance. The danger is that since the anxieties defended against are primitive and violent, defences may also be primitive. A social defence system develops over time as the result of collusive interaction and agreement, often unconscious, between members of the group as to what form it shall take. The socially structured defence mechanisms then tend to become an aspect of external reality with which all members of the group must come to terms.

In regard to large study groups and the use of social defences, I have in mind a large study group in which, in spite of the professional consultancy, my colleagues and I were unable to get the group to consider any differences; it was a truly homogenised group. Members were totally and utterly stuck in a social system against the anxiety of being in a large group. This was so powerful that nothing that I or my colleagues tried to do created any movement in the group. All attempts failed, none of the consultants could work with them.

This was an excellent example of the experience of the group being in a ba freezing state, as described earlier.

Projective identification

I now want to show how the mechanisms of projective and introjective identification operate in linking individual and social behaviour. Projective identification is an important process that enables us to understand a wide range of group and organisational phenomena. As consultants we need to understand how this defence mechanism can influence group and organisational behaviour. Projective identification is a frequent occurrence between two or more persons or groups whereby one person projects certain unwanted mental contents onto and into another person or group, with a resulting alteration in the behaviour of the targeted person. It is not just a mechanism of projection since it also affects another person.

Projective identification refers to efforts by persons to rid themselves of certain mental contents by depositing unwanted feelings into another's feeling system. The first person wishing to get rid of an unwanted feeling treats the other as if they had or embodied the feeling state. The way in which the recipient of this process responds has an important impact on the experience of the sender. If the recipient simply enacts the role he is assigned, then a tacit, collusive agreement is established in which the original meaning of the unwanted feelings or fantasies is reinforced and the defence against thinking about them confirmed. It will be recalled that if we want to feel "good" about ourselves, then "not me" has to be "bad". We need the other to confirm we are not like that. Thus, the scapegoat takes on or accentuates the characteristics attributed to him and confirms the repugnance the others feel for that (disowned) aspect. Perhaps a member embodies the role assigned by the group, such as the rebellion leader.

The unconscious transfer of information that occurs via projective identification is primarily a two-phase process. It begins with the denial and ejection of (unwanted) feelings which are inherent in a person's unconscious image (fantasy) of a situation. Members of a large group deal with their unbearable thoughts and feelings by splitting them off and locating them in other individuals or subgroups, including the consultants. In the second phase of projective identification, the recipient of the attribution or projection is essentially inducted into the originator's scheme of things. Thus, they are subtly pressured into thinking, feeling, and behaving in a manner congruent with the feelings or thoughts evacuated by the others.

Thus, while projective identification is a defensive process in the sense of unconsciously serving to insulate the projector from an aspect of his experience, it is a mode of communication in the sense that the feelings which are congruent with one's own inner image are induced in another, creating a sense of "being understood by or at one with the other". As various group members or subgroups come to symbolise or represent some unwanted aspect, they can serve as repositories for certain projected-out elements, and are then induced to enact these feelings or phantasies. The often-observed patterns of role differentiation in which groups pressure a member into a needed role, and scapegoating, are comprehensible in terms of projective identification.

Concluding remarks

The large group is the one event, apart from the opening plenary and the ending discussion group, in which members can experience the forces that a large group brings to bear on its leaders, in a setting where the prescribed task is to study those forces. Because the large group contains the total membership, it is the first event to end on the last day, and thus offers an appropriate preparation for ending. It provides the first experience of the need for mourning.

It is the event in which the individual finds that he has to take personal responsibility for his actions. If he is to behave in a mature and adult manner, he cannot just dissolve into the group, but has to accept the responsibility for stopping something of which he disapproves, or the guilt of not doing so. But to get to this realisation he has to be prepared to examine many of the myths and value systems he has previously accepted with few questions: that the "goodness" or "badness" of groups depends entirely on the "goodness" or "badness" of the individuals who make them up; that on matters of principle, majorities and minorities have very much relevance; that structure and leadership are always positive and not, as they are found to be, defence against anxiety. He has to be prepared to question many of the beliefs and attitudes that in a complex modern society support most of its social, political, and working institutions. He has to face the difficulty of tolerating uncertainty about outcomes and the inability always to understand human affairs. He also has to learn to recognise that, in the chaotic complexity in which so much of human life is lived, simple solutions provided by dogmatic leaders work only if the reality of the complexity is denied.

Aside from any other learning, members develop the important learning that it is not possible to create a work group in a large-group setting. In one such group that I was consulting to, a member realised the significance of this learning. He explained that the previous day he had asked colleagues to invite a large number of members of his organisation to a meeting, but had now cancelled it.

CHAPTER 5

The inter-group (IG) event—(day 3)

The inter-group event

The task of the inter-group (IG) event is to study relationships between groups as they develop and to exercise the task of giving and taking authority. The primary task of this event is to learn from the opportunities provided for members to explore the interpersonal and inter-group dynamics, and to study the behaviour of groups; and between groups, as it happens.

The inter-group event starts in plenary, chaired by the IG director, with three other members of staff, who have been delegated consultancy roles, being present. In the IGO group relations conferences the IG event is scheduled for day three. It has four one-and-a-half-hour sessions, including the opening plenary. The number of rooms available is governed by the number of members and number of consultants. A usual IG event will have about thirty members, and there will be four rooms available. Three for the groups to work in with a consultant, and the plenary room.

The plenary room is available for all meetings between groups and representatives of groups. Members of groups may visit the other groups in their room but only to convey messages and to arrange meetings in the plenary room.

The director of the IG event (usually the deputy director) will be consulting to all inter-group activities in the plenary room (perhaps with a training colleague), and three other consultants will be available in the three other rooms. The IG director will tell the members that in a moment he will ask the members to form their groups of more or less equal size of their choice, but they may not be the SSG or RAG groups. The members will then choose the room (the territory) for each group. But first the IG director will need to provide a little more about the focus of study.

In this event there are two tasks, as explained below:

1. The LEARNING TASK—here the focus of study is on the inter-play between the internal relations and preoccupations of your own group; and your external relations with the other groups. This task will give you opportunities to learn from the process of selecting your groups; and from how each group structures itself to engage in the inter-group task. For example: by managing boundaries, selecting representatives, exercising authority on behalf of others, and from handling leadership and followership issues. You may also learn from exploring and testing out the beliefs and assumptions that develop about the other groups.
2. The PRACTICAL TASK is to negotiate and engage in inter-group activity that will be helpful to your learning. Each group needs to agree on what, from your experience of selecting and forming your group, and working together, will be helpful learning to offer to the other group. For example, this may include issues of authority, lead-ership, competition, and beliefs and assumptions about the other group that you have experienced, which might be helpful to share and test out.

To complete this PRACTICAL TASK each group will need to decide who will be delegated and authorised to represent the group; and a meeting arranged between representatives in the plenary room.

Representatives will then return to their own groups to give feed-back of their experiences of representatives going and returning, and of others staying and working on their behalf. Then each group might want to consider a response to the experience of meeting with the other group, and to consider further inter-group activity.

During the inter-group event, the groups may authorise their members to act on their behalf outside their territory, in one or both of the following roles:

- Representative—who is authorised and delegated to interact with the other group, within the limits of specific instruction or area of authority or responsibility. The representative is sent out to deliver a message, express a point of view, or take an action on behalf of his own group, but has no discretion to vary the allotted task.
- Plenipotentiary—a representative with full authority to act and make decisions on behalf of the group.

The role of consultant in this event is not to teach or manage, but to provide consultancy to each group in the process of working to the inter-group task; and to offer observations and hypotheses about the processes and dynamics which may be occurring.

The IG director will then inform the members that he is going to repeat the above so that they may make notes if they wish to; but first, do they have any questions? If there are questions, they will be responded to.

The IG director will then ask the consultants to go to their rooms.

The IG director will then repeat the previous information and then invite the members to form three groups.

Before the arrival of the groups at the rooms delegated to the consultants, they will ensure that the room is not set up in any particular way, leaving it to the group to arrange the seating however they wish. The consultants will set up their own chairs so that they are not likely to be included in the group, when they arrive.

Selection of groups

Having spent the previous day in large-group sessions where homogeneity has played a significant role, the members may face a conflict between securing membership of a group and wanting to get out of the large group that is in this room, as soon as possible. How the groups form is highly significant as to how the groups will develop. It is frequently the case that those members with a strong valency, who have taken up or been mobilised into leadership roles on days one and two, will offer themselves up as leaders and invite others to form a group with them. These may be narcissistic or autocratic members who want to be powerful during the group's formation process. It is not unusual for small subgroups to transfer their loyalty from one forming group to another. As the process continues, some members may be feeling rejected, abandoned, and unwanted and will join any group that will have them. Indeed, while two of the groups may have formed reasonably quickly and gone off to choose a room, the third group may be hesitant and struggling to come together, but are left to go with what there is and to go to the only room left available.

Working groups often try to select their members based on some idea of competence: Who might be a useful and productive member of this team? Who could take up effectively the various tasks required for this kind of work: the organiser as leader? Other groups, often informal, are created around the idea of sentience, involving preferences, tastes, common interests, affections: Whom do I like? Whom do I want to spend time with? If they are lucky, competence and sentience will overlap: they may enjoy the company of their colleagues at work and carry out their joint tasks more effectively for that reason.

In reality, while the above considerations may be present in the unconscious wishes of members, they are seldom at the front of the forming of the groups. A likely occurrence is that the organiser assumes a leadership role, hoping that this will be acceptable to the other members.

Power and authority

Having spent the two previous days working in small and large groups, and struggling to cope with unfamiliar tasks and developing new understanding, the members may experience the IGO as a welcome opportunity to work in a much more familiar manner. However, such is the nature of the tasks involved, and the absence of any form of formal authority and structure, that it soon becomes obvious that this may also be a highly demanding experience. Issues of power and authority soon come to the fore and are affected by the emotional and unconscious processes. Consequently, it is important that as consultants to the processes occurring in this event, all consultants need to have an understanding of the dynamics that are likely to occur.

Whether we like it or not, it is impossible to escape the notion of power and authority. Any cursory reflection on our history will show us that natural social groups have developed in the form of families, clans, tribes, states, and nations. Within these groups, superior and subordinate relationships have developed in the form of status and role systems. Based on any number of characteristics, power structures evolve naturally, and they in turn are perpetuated by tradition. Indeed, it may be hard to imagine that the human community could proceed in its endeavours without an institutionalised power structure, which we call authority. However, as in so many similar conceptual frameworks, what is required is a workable compromise.

On the one hand, we need enough authority to ensure cooperative action and progress towards group goals. But on the other hand, we also want to encourage individuality, creativity, and innovation. At one extreme, anarchy is inconceivable; but so is the other extreme, authoritarianism. It might be helpful in considering these extremes if we bear in mind the distinctions between power and authority. These are frequently used as interchangeable concepts but I would suggest that this can only lead to confusion and emotional strife.

Taking a fairly traditional view of power we can say that it is basically a capacity that one person has to influence the behaviour of another person or persons so that the other person or persons do something that they would not otherwise have done. This would seem to imply that power is a potential that needs to be exercised to be effective and that it relies upon a dependence relationship. Various sources and bases of power have been identified; some of these are as follows: reward power; knowledge power; coercive power; position power; personal power; expert power; and opportunity power. In short, we might consider all of these under the heading of "resource power"; at different times and at different places the resource will vary from, say, reward to expertise or whatever, but it all seems to come back to the resources of the powerful.

"Authority" may be seen as a neutral term, but such is the emotion surrounding the exercise of authority that there are many misconceptions. A common error is for authority to be confused with both influence and authoritarianism. In effect, "authority" means that the person or persons with authority have the sole right to do anything within the terms of their authority. This is in contrast to influence, which may be effected over any area but the influencer may have to make reference to someone or something else for the necessary approvals. In other words, influence (and the power that may engender), may not be coexistent with authority.

Moving now to authoritarianism, this is simply a particular kind of authority that exists at the expense of freedom. On the one hand, authoritarianism results from an obsession with hierarchical relationships to the degree that superiors eschew consultation with subordinates. But on the other hand, subordinates are disposed towards zealous obedience to hierarchic superiors. Thus, we may end up with a collusive dynamic leading to authoritarianism.

As with power, to gain a deeper understanding of authority, it will help to explore something of its sources and foundations. In practice, authority—the right to carry out task leadership—stems from various sources. The most obvious, and most often related to, is the notion of authority as institutionalised power, which is established legally to achieve the objectives of a formal organisation. It is based on legal foundations, for example, legislation, articles of incorporation, partnership agreements, and bye-laws that define an organisation's mission and empower its members to carry out its activities. The fountainhead of all authority in a private enterprise such as a partnership is the owner(s), and in a corporation, it is the shareholders. It is they who delegate the authority to managers and leaders and, most importantly, set the boundaries of that authority. What we are referring to here is "managerial authority" which refers to that part of the leader's authority that has been delegated to them by the institution they work in.

In many organisations the extent and details of this sort of authority are contained in a job description and perhaps a job specification. These documents, taken together, formally set out the boundaries of the authority which is being delegated to the individual manager. Whatever the job description may be, it is important to understand that it concerns authority for matters which have been delegated by someone who, in turn, has the right to delegate that degree of authority. We may conclude, therefore, that authority is the application of power by the manager as a means of political action which is aimed at following and achieving goals linked to the organisation's primary task. Authority may thus be considered functional and rationally related to organisational functioning. Power used by a manager in support of achieving organisational goals and tasks is legitimate and in the interests of the organisation.

As has already been stated, power as influence may be affected over any area but if it is to be legitimately used the influencer may have to make reference to someone or something else for the necessary approvals. In other words, influence may not be coexistent with authority. Where power is used outside the legitimate boundaries of authority, it may be considered an abuse of power. Using power in a political sense of organisational functioning we can say that where behaviour is carried out by individuals or groups in the pursuit of individual interests or goals, such as an attempt to influence other members to do something contrary to the aims of the group, this will be an abuse of authority. In that regard, institutional politics may be considered a form of rivalry, a challenge to the legitimate authority of the group, to determine which members of the group are most powerful—a classic power struggle. In like manner, where an individual uses power in an authoritarian manner that impinges on the freedom of others, this is equally an illegitimate use of and an abuse of power.

However, while the foregoing may be held in the mind of members in the IGO event, there is no question of formal authority being available to the group. The task of the group is to develop a form of structure that will enable them to work at the stated tasks. In this respect, there is but one source of power: "leadership authority". This is very different and refers to that aspect of the manager's or leader's authority that is derived from the recognition of other group members that they have the capacity to carry out the task. Here, I am defining "leadership" as always involving attempts on the part of the leader (influencer) to affect (influence) the behaviour of a follower.

However, I have to confess to a degree of discomfort with the term "follower". My discomfort is with the connotation of a set and determined hierarchical relationship between *the* leader and their followers. I have in mind a picture of the manager being *the* leader, the one with all the knowledge, the one with all the ideas, and the followers being expected to thank the leader profusely and blindly follow whatever they say. This is getting very close to the notion of the authoritarian leader who ignores the freedom of others. I much prefer to think of leaders and "joiners": of any member of the team leading on a particular issue and others (including the manager) joining them to further consider and build on the idea that the team member seeks to influence them about.

Leadership authority differs from management authority in a highly significant way. Management authority is clearly delegated to the manager only. He can delegate responsibility for this authority but the manager and only the manager is still accountable for performance. In the IG we are concerned in regard to leadership authority that this can rest with the leader but it does not have to. Any member of the group can take their authority for leadership. Indeed, in any group that values their personnel then all will be encouraged to take on leadership authority.

Managerial and leadership authority reinforce each other; both are, in turn, dependent upon other sources of authority: such as the leader's technical knowledge, their personality, their human skills, and the social tasks and responsibilities they assume outside the organisation. The leader is responsible not only to the group but also to the other members, to their professional and ethical values, to the conference as a whole; responsibility and accountability represent the reciprocal obligation of the leader to the sources of their authority. The group structure can be considered functional when the distribution and delegation of authority, task performance, and task monitoring are matched by appropriate, that is, sufficient and stable but not excessive, investment of authority in the leader.

The true nature of authority is that the leader is able to directly affect the behaviour of a member of an organisation if they possess authority with respect to that member. But the real source of authority possessed by a group leader lies in the acceptance of its exercise by those who are subject to it. A group leader may have the authority to tell members how to carry out their task or what to do but it is the members who determine the authority which the leader may wield. In effect, authority only becomes real when it is accepted. No matter what the leader may tell them to do, or demand that they do, it may all be in vain. A leader can only use authority if it is accepted by the other team members. Thus, to be effective, the members define the useful limits of the leader's authority. We may usefully summarise the situation with the slogan: "leadership is nothing without followership (or joiners)".

Faced with an authoritative leader, staff may find it such an unbearable experience that they identify with the aggressor and become like the bullying leader. In this case, the whole group may ride roughshod over those inside or outside the group that they have relationships with. Apart from the obvious result of poor relationships and bad reputation, there is another more important outcome. Identification with the aggressor means giving up certain aspects of self and repressing them into our unconscious. The mental conflict caused by adopting behaviour that is not really acceptable will put a considerable strain on those concerned and sickness may be a result. The unbearable thoughts and feelings arising from being bullied may also be dealt with by other defence mechanisms. However, where workers or staff are able to stay in touch with reality, where they refuse to be bullied, where they take their own authority to not respond to a manager who is abusing his power by acting outside his authority, the bully may be left with no authority.

In most instances the leaders may, on the face of things, have immense authority. They may have the right to reward and punish members without referral to anyone else. But, in practice, although they may demand or insist, there is no guarantee that other members will fully comply. The concept of "authority" then, describes an interpersonal relationship in which one individual, the group member, accepts a decision made by another individual, the leader, permitting that decision directly to affect their behaviour. A group member always has an opportunity, with respect to a decision made by the leader directly to affect his behaviour, to accept or reject that decision. It is appreciated, of course, that such rejection by the group member may result in dismissal, or at the very least, the need for a voluntary leaving.

Thus far, this has been a fairly traditional exploration of power and authority. But we have already been alerted to some of the difficulties that may arise from behaviour beneath the surface. To appreciate just how important the notion of authority is we only have to reflect on the fact that we all start our lives dependent on authority figures. We can, therefore, begin to have an appreciation of the likely effect that authority will have on all of us throughout our lives. Starting our lives dependent on authority figures can have a lasting influence on our relationships and relatedness to other authority figures that we come across in later life. If the authority figure, the father or the mother, is experienced, introjected, and becomes an internal object that is feared or disliked for some reason, our meaning-making process regarding future experiences of authority figures may be to see them as feared or disliked.

Seen in the light of the problems of identity, the "me" may bring to the relationship with his leader the belief that he is oppressed, insecure, and looking to the leader to make most major decisions. In addition, they may seek to project into the leader feelings of competence and power so that he acts in an overpowering manner, the beneath-the-surface processes being unconsciously designed to ensure that previously expected conditions are replicated in the current situation.

Where we have experienced a parent as controlling and perhaps aggressive, we may develop a mental image of an authority figure possessing all these qualities and this mental image will be associated with all the feelings that helped to create that image. As a young child, we may have been terrified that we were forever going to be berated and slapped down on every occasion that we attempted to assert our freedom. And on the occasions that this occurred, we may have suffered extreme feelings of frustration, anger, and even murderous thoughts regarding the object that was doing the controlling. When later in life we are confronted with a leader that triggers these feelings, we may treat that person as if they were the parent.

I feel sure that all who are managers have experienced a group member who no matter what the circumstances always has a valency that seems to be difficult and uncooperative. Seen in a non-reflective way, the leader may simply consider this as a personal matter and that the member of staff simply does not like him. However, if we are able to gain an understanding of beneath-the-surface processes, we may consider that relationships with the group member may be evoking feelings developed with a significant other from a previous relationship. And this is why the group member responds in such a difficult manner. If we are non-reflective, we can view him as an object that is synonymous with the behaviour of a difficult person; or if we are reflective, as a person who is sometimes difficult. This latter approach may eventually result in changed behaviour by the employee.

Beneath the adult struggles with power, right, and legitimacy, there remain these archaic images of what strength and power should be, so that as adults we are interpreting not what is really occurring now but what once was in our lives. It is rather like reading a hidden text with more powerful messages. What happened to us in childhood is that every action of our parents contributed to our image of their strength. The infant has no standards for judgement, no way of separating his self from the parent; whatever the parent does is potent, and the infant cannot imagine, in what is an egoistic universe, that the parent does anything which has no effect on that young self. Is Mummy depressed? It must be my fault. Is Daddy angry? It must be because of something I have done. When they punish me, I don't understand the reasons, but I must have been bad. Do they love me? Then they must love me absolutely.

At a later stage, the child simply competes with the parent of the same sex, a competition with a naturally ambivalent outcome (the Oedipus complex). The little boy wants to take the place of his father, but does not want to lose his father's love. At later stages, adolescents divorce themselves from obedience to their parents, but nonetheless want the parents to care for them whenever they are in need. An adult would come to admit the strength as well as the limits of his parents, but would see the strength on its own terms, as a force which belonged to them, made him, but is now not part of his own. This is all part and parcel of developing personality boundaries. This does not mean that as adults we shall always be able to make decisions that are totally free of other people. For example, in the work situation, an individual may find the leader's approach totally abhorrent and would have a strong need to challenge him. However, a stronger need may be to remain working with the group. In these circumstances, by means of denial, he may blot out the feelings associated with his leader.

In all authority relationships there are likely to be difficulties. In almost every situation that involves hierarchical relationships, each individual's unique personality is of paramount importance in the way they will respond to those seeking to exercise power and authority. Each unique individual will bring their own meaning-making self to the situation, and this will affect the relationships. By way of example, a manager or friend may seek to offer a helping hand to someone by offering advice and support in achieving a task. Unknown to the helper, when the person was young, he had experienced the father deserting him and the rest of the family; a result being that this caused the child to see all male authority figures as "bad" and "not to be trusted". Faced with someone who triggers their unconscious image of father they treat the "helper" as if they are the father. They put into practice their tried and tested plans for dealing with untrustworthy authority figures which might involve espousing agreement but choosing to ignore the advice.

Intra-group dynamics—leadership, authority, and delegation

By way of example, we might consider the activities of a group functioning as a work group and the several identifiable processes that characterise such a group.

In recognition of a task, this small group must develop a structure if it is to operate effectively. This begins with a boundary, delineating inside from outside: "This individual is a member of our group, our team—he can come in. This one is not—he will have to stay outside." Second, the territory needs to be marked out, the chairs need to be set in a way that the members can work as a work group (conscious, working to task, collaborative). Members will come from several different backgrounds and organisational experiences. What all will have experienced in common are the formal structures and delegated roles that are normal to their organisations. Here, they are plunged into a situation where there is no formal structure or roles. To be effective, to be a work group, they need to develop a structure and roles.

I am always surprised at how very quickly a group of people coming together in the way described above, if fortunate to have selected and authorised a competent leader, become an identifiable group, seeing the group as *our* group and beginning to assume they are better than the other groups. However, a group not being so fortunate to have a competent leader, will struggle to become an identifiable group, because of a lack of agreed structure. (See pp. 23–27 for more on GRC structure.)

Leadership

In the IG, there is never going to be any formal authority granted to any member to be the leader of the group. This makes it important that he should seek leadership authority from all members. This may present a problem for the self-appointed leader who has a strong valency. They may be determined to hold on to their newly gained power, reluctant to lose control, fear failure, fear rejection, fear loss of power. Seeking authority may feel like giving up on their plans. Equally, discussion among the members around the issue of a need for a leader may be very informative; for example, they may suggest the need for a facilitator, that is, someone with no power. It will be a clear indication that they are not prepared to act as followers to this self-appointed leader. Without authority, this person cannot remain the leader.

Being a leader inevitably means giving and taking authority; which often creates all manner of conflict and competition. Not least, the members may now be wanting to challenge the self-authorised leader, others wanting to become leader, especially if the leader has failed to consider and provide the basic requirements stated above, leaving the small group as a disorganised bunch of individuals. No one in the group has genuine authority for anything, and there is no provision for a process of decision making; instead, the fallback position is the non-decision of decision-making being done by whole-group decisions. In the absence of formal authority, nothing can change. Members become anxious and want to become active. Self-appointed members say they want to arrange meetings. Others wander off to visit other groups. Consultants are largely ignored. The self-appointed leader becomes more and more autocratic, they don't know what to do but don't want to give up their position.

The exercise of power and authority will frequently evoke feelings of competition. Groups and organisations may evoke feelings of sibling rivalry or simply those concerning our desires to gain favourable responses from our mother. Authority and decision-making in groups and organisations require that authority needs to be taken by the leader and that others must, in turn, give their authority to the leader. Where this is not possible because of the competitive dynamics existing in the group or organisation, there is likely to be stagnation, no progress, and no decisions or perhaps more accurately no real decisions. Competition can prevent the giving or taking of authority; for example, an individual may withhold their authority because, although they may not express the desire, at an unconscious level they want to be the leader.

Where competition is not confronted and remains unresolved, it may result in self-exclusion and/or exclusion of others. For example, where members of the group are attempting to work together as a work group, and several members are highly competitive and unconsciously seek to be the leader in opposition to the appointed leader, the group will be unable to operate as a group. The highly competitive members who fail to authorise the appointed leader will exclude themselves and probably the other members of the group who support them. I have often heard managers talking enthusiastically about "healthy competition" being good for a group. Taking a reflective stance, I am much more concerned that beneath-the-surface processes concerning competition may be extremely unhealthy for the group and its members.

Where a leader is not supported, he suffers the painful feeling of rejection and may seek to sabotage other members' attempts to lead. Frequently, the number of challengers may reduce to three members, two of whom have strong support from other group members, and the third is regarded as a weak candidate. The usual way to resolve this competition is for the group members to vote. Because of the strong backing for the two strong candidates, members will not change their voting intentions, meaning that neither will be elected. However, members who supported both strong candidates may have changed their votes and supported the weak candidate. So, this person becomes the leader by default. This is unlikely to be sustainable, and competition is likely to continue.

Consultants may point out that there is no leadership, the group has no decision-making process, and there is competition which prevents any work regarding the task. Sadly, this may have no effect because the group dynamics are now lacking in any form of authority. I once consulted to such a group for two whole sessions in a morning. During lunch, I made a decision that I would tell the group what needed to be done to avoid a whole day of no learning. When the next session started, I told the group that if there was to be any learning, some of those competing for the leadership needed to agree to be followers of a leader. This resulted in two agreeing that in the interests of learning, they would be followers. Another, who had been competing, recommended that a woman who had no interest in being leader be accepted as the leader. This was supported by all, who saw this woman as not being a competitor. This freed the group sufficiently for decisions being made to work to the tasks.

This example raises a serious question: was I out of role, had I been unconsciously mobilised to rescue the group from its predicament? The answer, in this instance, is a very firm, no. I was fully conscious of what I was doing, and was acting in accordance with my philosophy that everything we do should be done for the benefit of the learning of the members.

Authority

We are never totally independent, even after "me" and "not me" have been established. As in the maternal and family holding environment, we are ambivalent about authority. At one level, we are always in danger of regressing to the comfortable dependent position. I feel certain that many of us can reflect on situations when we simply did not support the relevant authority figure, yet we decided to go along with them for an easy life. At another level, we are at once ravenous for the comfort of a stronger person and in a rage against the very strength they so desire. Given the infant's journey from dependency to individuation this may not be surprising. The ambivalent nature of this struggle between a sense of freedom and the fear of abandonment is likely to be repeated and experienced in later situations. Thus, we may welcome the strong leader for providing a framework for our support, but we may reject this same strong leader because they are interfering with our sense of freedom.

In effect, what people are willing to believe is not simply a matter of the credibility or legitimacy of the ideas, rules, and persons offered to them. It is also a matter of them needing to believe. What they want from an authority is as important as what the authority has to offer. Where there is a great deal of anxiety and dependence, they may seek out a leader who offers them the security of a way out of their discomfort. In this sort of situation, those concerned may be vulnerable to a leader intent on abusing the power afforded him by the dependent others. In this way, we may be attracted to strong figures even if they are not legitimate. This is a collusive process whereby an assumed leader who is obsessed with maintaining total control is supported in this use of power by others who are disposed towards zealous obedience to hierarchic superiors. It is in this way that we may end up with a collusive dynamic leading to authoritarianism. Anyone who has a knowledge of the situation in Germany in the 1930s will be aware that this is precisely how Hitler and the Nazi Party came to power with such horrific results. Doubtless, we may be able to recall other relevant examples in organisations and institutions.

The authority situation between group members is always likely to recreate, to some extent, in those involved, a dependency situation analogous to one's infancy and will thus tend to reactivate the characteristic way of handling problems which was developed at that time. As the child sought help from their parents, a group member seeks help and assistance from their leader. Even a simple request for something like a favourable agreement of authority to be a delegate places the group member in a subordinate position from a person in authority. When the help requested is more extensive than this, the feeling of dependency is proportionately greater. It is impossible for members of groups to place themselves for long in such a dependency situation without there being some level of transference to this new situation of their infantile attitudes. Part of this transference will be positive, corresponding to the love felt for the parental figure; part of it will be negative, corresponding to the fear of anyone possessing such power over one's own destiny.

I have thus far mainly concentrated on those who are subjected to authority: those who are being managed or influenced. I now want to refer to those who are taking authority. Taking personal or collective authority can be a very anxiety-provoking situation. Making a wrong decision may have most serious reputational implications in human terms. Thus, environmental circumstances will always influence the behaviour of those in authority.

Past influences on those taking authority will also be important. For example, I have referred briefly to those who may abuse power, especially those who seek to control others in an authoritarian manner.

This, of course, is not the only category of person who is in the position of exercising power and authority. There will be a wide range of individuals who will all be influenced by their unique personality. This may include those who are guided by an internal world that seeks to encourage cooperation and the avoidance of conflict in a way that corresponds to the love felt for the parental figure.

People fear exercising power when they do not have a sufficiently good internal image of their character, when they feel they are fundamentally "bad"; and if they feel they are partly bad and mean, they are reluctant to wield power, fearing that they will be unable to contain their anger and will therefore hurt others and be hurt in turn. Aggression and power conjure up an imagined world where people persecute one another. In psychological terms, we can say that such persons have too punishing or too harsh a superego, a conscience that is too strict and constantly reprimands them for the smallest misdeeds or for simply bad or forbidden thoughts. An example may be a situation where a group is constantly failing to achieve at the level required. The leader is angry, frustrated, and concerned that things have to change. However, instead of expressing his feelings in an assertive manner, he simply sympathises with their predicament. He is scared that he will become violent and aggressive and will, therefore not exercise his authority.

Delegation

I have great difficulty in distinguishing between leaders and managers. The most widely accepted definition of a manager is someone who gets things done through other people. That is what management is all about. It is the ability to delegate that distinguishes the good manager from the bad. The manager who utilises the skills, aptitudes, and commitment of his subordinates to develop them and broaden their experience is the one most likely to succeed. What separates management winners from management losers? What secret enables successful managers to meet great expectations with limited resources? What tool virtually defines the successful manager? It is the ability to delegate.

We might ask, how could an ability to delegate make such a difference? It is simply because delegation is the most important of all managerial skills. It is, in fact, the skill that defines a manager. A manager is someone who gets things done through people. Delegation is nothing more than accomplishing results through the efforts of others. It is the manager's most basic and important tool.

Group leaders who delegate effectively will find that the quality of their own work will steadily grow. They will also find that the group will start to run much more smoothly. The work of the members will be greatly enhanced by virtue of a greater variety of tasks being passed down to them. Because they are undertaking broader tasks, the group members will derive more satisfaction from their work and will almost certainly do a better job simply because they are enjoying the challenge of new demands on their capabilities.

Because they are deriving more fulfilment from their work, they can be expected to be working to task. They are bound to invest more effort in enriching work than into the dull routine of the repetitive tasks they have been performing for a long time. These benefits are likely to ensure working to task throughout the group. In addition, the members will recognise the considerable degree of trust the delegating leader is showing in their capabilities and will feel they are a more significant part of the group. This can only enhance the sense of esprit de corps and create the kind of relationships under which group work and the striving for excellence flourish.

If delegation is done for the right reasons, it can be a powerful and enriching tool that benefits leader and group members alike. If the intention is simply to pass on unwanted tasks, the true benefits of delegation will be wasted. The more enlightened approach is that delegation should be used to enrich the roles of group members by stretching them and broadening their experience. In this way, they will grow in the role and help facilitate effective performance. A fully developed group member will have achieved learning and is also likely to be more committed and motivated.

You will recall that delegation is an important part of the learning task in the IG. This task will give members opportunities to learn from the process of selecting groups; and from how each group structures itself to engage in the inter-group task; for example, by managing boundaries, selecting representatives, exercising authority on behalf of others, and from handling leadership and followership issues. When it comes to inter-group activity, delegation is a highly significant learning experience.

The role of the consultants

The role of the consultants is to provide consultancy to the total membership and individual groups and to offer observations and hypotheses about the processes and dynamics which may be occurring. In IGO conferences, the consultants introduce themselves to the newly created groups and then inform them of their role. They will tell the members: the process we adopt is not teaching in the traditional sense. In other words, don't expect the consultants to be doing all the usual things that a teacher or trainer normally does. The role of staff is to provide the structure for learning and to provide observations or hypotheses about what they feel is happening at any given moment that may assist the members in their learning. Everything the consultants do will be done for the benefit of the learning of the members.

Taking up my role as a consultant to a group in a territory, I would normally tell the group from the beginning that the director of this event has delegated authority to me to be the consultant to the people in this room. A word about my role as consultant: a) I'm not a member of the group; b) I'm not a trainer; and c) I'm not going to be taking a management role. Management, structure, and issues of authority are entirely a matter for the members of the group in this room to consider as you develop in pursuing learning regarding the internal relations and preoccupations of your group and your external relations with other groups. My role as a consultant is to analyse the activities of the group and to either respond to requests for assistance by the members of the group, or to offer observations and hypotheses about what is happening in the group at any given time, that would invite the group to consider how things might be done more effectively. I'm not here to create a dependency relationship with you, but everything I do will be done for the benefit of your learning. In this respect, you might like to consider that I am to be seen as a helpful resource for your learning.

From the foregoing, it may be appreciated that a consultant to an IG group requires experience in the role of an organisational consultant. Those who have not had the benefit of this experience may be fortunate as training consultants to work with an organisation consultant and to learn from his knowledge, skill, and ability. In addition, there will always be further opportunities at CPD sessions. The reading of these chapters will also be helpful references.

First staff meeting

At the end of the first session, the IG director will chair a meeting of all staff. The first item is to establish where all members are located. The director will describe the way that the group formed the three groups. The three consultants to groups will then share who the members are in each group. They will then describe what progress each of the groups has made in creating a structure in the groups they are consulting to. Some groups may have authorised a doorkeeper to manage the boundary; they may have the self-appointed leader, who may or may not be secure in that role. Other groups may still be struggling in the process of coming to agreement regarding anything to do with structure. The emphasis, at this stage, has been on the study of the interplay between the internal relations and preoccupations of each group. It is unlikely, at this stage, that any group has been able to consider the practical task of negotiating and engaging in inter-group activity.

At the end of the second session, the IG director will again chair a meeting of all staff. The three consultants to groups will then describe the further progress that each of the groups has made in creating a structure in the groups they are consulting to. If a group has created a reasonable structure that permits leadership, sound decision-making procedures, and clear delegation, it may have started to move from intra-group activity to inter-group activity. If groups are still having problems of competition for leadership, failure to give authority, and followership, or decision-making, they will inevitably still be engaged with intra-group dynamics and not be able to even begin to consider inter-group activity. The director and staff will discuss how consultancy could be helpful to their respective groups.

Depending on the progress of the IG groups, the IG director in the large room will soon be having representatives of groups notifying arranged meetings and time.

Here, the groups are beginning to consider the practical task. Each group needs to agree on what, from its experience of selecting and forming the group, and working together, will be helpful learning for the other groups. This may include those matters that have been discussed above: issues of forming groups, leadership and followership, structure, competition, and beliefs and assumptions about the other groups that they have experienced, which might be helpful to explore and test out.

In regard to the inter-group activity, there are the two roles described earlier:

- Representative—who is authorised and delegated to interact with the other group, within the limits of specific instruction or area of authority or responsibility. The representative is sent out to deliver a message, express a point of view, or take an action on behalf of his own group, but has no discretion to vary the allotted task.
- Plenipotentiary—the plenipotentiary represents the group in a much fuller way than a delegate. He is a representative sent out with flexible terms of reference, including negotiation, although these terms of reference might be contained within specific parameters.

Here, I will describe my taking up of the role of IG director.

I usually prepare seating for two members of the group calling the meeting, and two chairs for the group invited to the presentation.

The first thing I want to know is which group has called the meeting and for what purpose.

I then want to know which other group has been invited to the meeting and what it sees as the purpose.

I then ask the presenting group representative(s) to tell me what they have been authorised to do in the meeting; and how, or by whom, have they been authorised.

Frequently, they have no clear authority, and at times, are self-authorised to come to a meeting. I will then ask the same of the receiving group representative to tell me what they have been authorised to do in the meeting; and how, or by whom, have they been authorised.

Frequently, they too have no clear authority, and at times, are self-authorised to come to a meeting. This is a clear indication that this group has not successfully developed a structure that will enable it to work at the IG tasks. As a minimum, there needs to be clarity of authority, around decision-making, delegation, a form of leadership, and management of boundaries.

If that is the situation, I will tell them to return to their groups and seek the assistance of their consultant regarding the importance of learning regarding authority.

If they have been fully and correctly authorised, the meeting will continue in the presence of the IG director.

I may, at this stage, send messages back to the groups concerned such as "why is the group not using its consultant?" or "why is there a lack of trust in the group?"

These may be directed at specific groups; or may form a hypothesis about the whole event.

To complete the practical task a total of six meetings will be held.

After session three, the IG director will again chair a meeting of all staff. The three consultants to groups will then describe the further progress that each of the groups has made in creating a structure in the groups they are consulting to. At this stage, there have possibly been changes to structures in the light of understanding discovered about other groups, and the failures of successfully working to task.

The inter-group work in the groups

Each group may be seen as a system, as may each member delegated to agree a meeting, those delegated to represent the group in a meeting between groups, and those who have a purpose agreed and authorised by their groups; and it is also a meeting between two systems. Where the IG consultants see these meetings from a systems perspective, they may consult to the task of the need to work across boundaries. This may trigger several emotions, such as, envy, secrecy, pride, and consideration of assumptions about others that they need to test out.

Systems

It may be helpful to see the whole event from a systems perspective. Systems theory provides a means of studying organisations and their management in a way that facilitates analysis and synthesis in a complex and dynamic environment. It considers interrelationships among systems as well as interactions or relatedness between the system and its external environment. Using the concepts of systems theory allows us to consider individuals, organisations, small groups, and large groups all within the constraints of an external environmental system. Systems of various types are all around us. The body itself is a complex organism including the skeletal system, the circulatory system, the nervous system, and of course, the mental system. We may also come into daily contact with such phenomena as transportation systems, communication systems, and economic systems. It will thus be clear that we can use the notion of system in various ways.

We may define a system as an organised, unitary whole, composed of two or more interdependent parts, components, or subsystems and delineated by identifiable boundaries from its external environment. Breaking this down, we might start with the identification of a coherent whole. Clearly, a group might be seen as a system and parts of the conference, such as group one, group two, group three (or their adopted titles if they have them). All three groups might equally be seen as wholes or subparts of the group as a whole.

This type of group or social system is one where groupings of people are aware of and acknowledge their membership of the group. They are perhaps most distinguished by virtue of the emotional involvement with other members. Frequently, these groupings develop something of the characteristics of the family: tensions develop, alliances form and reform, and emotions colour the activities. Relating back to our exploration of the group as a whole, such a reaction is hardly surprising given the tendency for groups to evoke memories of, and behave as if they were part of, the maternal environment.

A basic premise is that a group, as a subsystem of the conference, must accomplish its goals within constraints that are an integral part of the external environment. A group is an open system that exchanges information and energy with its environment. In this view, groups are dependent for their survival on an exchange of information and communication with their environment. Environmental forces have a direct impact on the way the group structures its activities. The group performs a function for the conference; if it is to be successful in receiving inputs, it must conform to social constraints and requirements. Conversely, the group influences its external environment.

This may helpfully lead us to a systems view that sees groups as social and psychological subsystems. The social part of a group is concerned with the ways in which the tasks of the organisation are divided (differentiation) and with the coordination of these activities (integration).

In a formal sense, structure can be set forth by organisation charts. Indeed, it is not unusual for groups in the IG exercise to develop such a chart. This is a relatively simple subsystem that can also be further divided into reasonably clearly demarcated elements such as structure, strategy, and delegation.

When we move to the psychological subsystem, we will be aware that every organisation is composed of individuals and groups in interaction and that each will be influenced by psychological factors. These may consist of individual behaviour and motivation, status and role relationships, group dynamics, and other influence systems. They may also be affected by sentiments, beliefs and values, attitudes, hopes, expectations, and aspirations, their anxieties and defence mechanisms, the ideas and ways of thinking of these same people that both determine how they perceive the external realities and shape their actions towards them. These are phenomena of subjective experience located within the minds of group people. Each of these elements may be considered and analysed as a separate element of the subsystem. In addition, we shall need to consider the dynamics arising from the level of the group as a whole.

This is a much more difficult subsystem to define, and it is even more difficult to divide it up into its respective elements. Here we are referring to dynamic processes that are unique for each individual or group and for each unique activity. However, what it does do is to call our attention to the fact that in all individual and group interactions, the psychological subsystem will have a huge influence on the conference subsystem. These two subsystems, the external and internal worlds of people—are in continual interaction: what goes on in the minds of people is partly reactive to what happens around them, but is also very much proactive. People's ideas and ways of thinking influence the way they act upon their surroundings to bring about change in them.

This also leads us to consider that other wholes may not be as clearly defined. If we take the three groups in the IG, they may be perceived as a coherent whole by those in a particular group, but this may not be at all obvious to the others outside that system, in the other two groups. Most importantly for our purposes, taking a systems perspective provides us with an opportunity to identify and make sense of some of the informal social systems that are present in our group. In many instances, nothing on a structure chart will give an indication of this sort of system and those outside the system may not be aware of its existence. By taking a systems approach, we may be able to develop the concept of a social system which may lead to a deeper understanding of the dynamics of the group. When we take a group-as-a-whole perspective it is important that we are able to identify these informal social systems to enable us to discover what they are representing for the conference as a whole system. This is the role of the IG director consultant, who creates a hypothesis of the whole system.

As we have seen, a group can divide in any number of ways and subgroups may form for any manner of reasons. Boundaries are relatively easily defined in biological and physical systems—they are visible—but it is harder to define the sociological and psychological boundaries of human behaviour and social systems, such as groups. Their boundaries need to be defined in terms of activities or processes.

External influences can bring great pressure on leaders who sometimes need to devise responses merely to survive. For example, one group may discover that one of the other groups has been more effective and organised in most of their meetings. There has followed a huge restructuring of the group which has frequently resulted in previously suggested structures now being supported. At a social subsystem level this doubtless seemed a rational response to the perceived problems. However, at a psychological subsystem level this response has been viewed as unfavourable, as the original structure was perceived by group members as the minimum obligations that they were owed by the group for their loyalty, conformity, and effort.

The consequences are predictable: group members are angry at the unilateral breaking of the psychological contract, and at the same time insecure, having lost trust in the group. And their feelings of inequity are increased by the disproportionate benefits enjoyed by the leader, who is perceived as toadying to consultants. Moreover, many feel helpless in the absence of power to help them affect the situation. Overall, they have lost their previous feelings of commitment. But such issues of motivation and morale are vital since groups need effort and commitment to get work done and a willingness to take risks in pursuit of innovation. Here, again, we have a seemingly rational approach to problem-solving that has not taken into consideration the beneath-the-surface dynamics.

In the circumstances, it would not be surprising if an anti-task approach was taken by the members of the group.

To conclude, by using a systems approach, we may reconsider the way that members of groups set up psychological boundaries to contain anxiety. When members of groups face uncertainty and feel at risk, they set up psychological boundaries that violate pragmatic boundaries based on tasks with the sole aim of reducing anxiety. The boundary separates their psychological region of certainty from a broader region of uncertainty. Or put another way, they develop forms of behaviour that they feel are psychologically appropriate to them under the circumstances imposed on them by their environment.

There is so much commitment of groups in the IG exercise that the influence of unconscious processes and emotional responses may result in hurtful and painful experiences for members taking up roles or not being supported to take up roles. The commitment to action often results in groups all working through scheduled breaks, with members ignoring time boundaries; doubtless based on a desire to be the best group, and to be confirmed as best group by the consultants. It has been my experience that seldom has a group allocated space to specifically study the learning task. There is no scheduled space for a review of the IG, but the following review and application group will enable many members to reflect on the roles they've been mobilised into. In addition, the following discussion group will provide a review with the help of the consultants.

CHAPTER 6

Review and application groups (RAG)

The task of the review and application groups is to consider the relevance of conference learning to normal work situations. These groups provide an opportunity to further understand group-as-a-whole processes by members identifying significant roles, themes, and experiences from the main event of the day and applying learning to work situations.

The sessions are of one and a half hours each, and they are scheduled to take place every day, immediately after the main event of the days, and before the discussion groups.

Membership of these groups will be taken from the membership of the SSGs and will remain the same throughout the conference. Small study group (SSG) formation will take place avoiding members who are known to each other being placed in the same SSG. In the application groups, membership will be of members from the same organisations, or same work category (e.g. coaching, or HR). Thus, it's going to result in members having different group experiences. The formation of the review and application groups will, in itself, provide a form of application, by connecting members with their organisational or work roles.

The task of the consultant in this event is to facilitate the members' learning, by exploring organisational applications of learning. This is not a here-and-now group, rather, it's a there-and-then group. The consultant needs to stay in role by holding the members to the task of reviewing and applying their conference learning to their personal and work situations.

It's my firm belief that application is the most important purpose of any group relations conference. If members cannot apply their learning to their everyday lives, we have not succeeded in our task. It's also important to understand that everything that occurs in a group relations conference will also occur in the everyday life of other organisational and personal groups of which we are members. All learning is applicable to post-conference experiences. In this chapter, we will concentrate on review and application as experienced in the conference main events of each day.

We will then concentrate on post-conference, organisational applications of conference learning.

The IGO group relations method of working: review

It is important to help members maintain a focus on group-as-a-whole learning rather than on the individual. Group-as-a-whole learning about leadership, authority, and organisation is our field of study, and it is this learning—which is not available from any other process—that we provide members with the various opportunities to learn. In this event, we need to have the skills and competence to provide members with the ability to take their learning with them into the workplace. We need to maintain our focus on the group-as-a-whole dynamics, rather than individual learning. On occasion the latter may also occur; for example, group-as-a-whole learning may be about the mobilisation of an individual as a flight leader; but it may also provide learning for an individual, who has a strong valency, and is easily mobilised by the group. Where this learning occurs, so be it; although not the essential aim, it should not be disregarded.

The consultant process

At the start of the first application group, the consultant will point out that this is not a here-and-now event; and confirm this by asking members to identify themselves. He will then read out the task of this event, and then invite members to take five to ten minutes to individually reflect on the experience of the learning from the main event of the day. He will ask them to capture the group-as-a-whole dynamics that have occurred, and list them. This not only helps the learning but frees up members' thinking. An opening question to the group might be, therefore: "What do you recall as being the most significant group-as-a-whole role taken up in today's main event?" In other words, we are initially conducting a review of group-as-a-whole dynamics.

The less structured the review and application group is, the more open members are able to grapple with reviewing and applying their understanding of group as a whole processes.

It should be understood that unlike some of the other (non-IGO) group relations conference processes, in this model, members are not given individual slots of time to explore their individual learning. We are solely and primarily concerned with group-as-a-whole learning. When all have completed their reflections, all are asked to share their learning in public. Thus, all are involved. As they go through the review process, the consultant will try to identify the most significant roles taken up during the day. He will then invite the members to further explore what was happening.

On day one, the learning will be that described in Chapter 3, "The small study group". This will include: mobilisation of basic assumption leaders for dependency, fight–flight, and/or pairing; how members are unconsciously mobilised by the group as a whole; how this relates to members' valencies; why anxiety; and why the group as a whole becomes filled with anxiety and adopts group-as-a-whole leadership by mobilising members. As stated above, as a result of members being from different groups, there may be a helpful degree of curiosity between the members, which will increase the learning.

On day two, the learning will be that described in Chapter 4, "The large study group". This will include: threats to identity in the large group, further unconscious mobilisation of members as leaders to avoid painful experiences and anxiety; the violent nature of a large group; the ba freezing of large groups; the learning that it's not possible to achieve work-group learning in a large group.

On day three, the learning will be that described in Chapter 5, "The inter-group event". This will include: intra-group dynamics, while creating a structure that will enable the successful achievement of the learning and practical tasks; competition, delegation—giving and taking of authority, inter-group dynamics, assumptions regarding the other, and the need to test out assumptions.

On day four, the learning will be about group-as-a-whole dynamics throughout the conference; large- and small-group processes. It will include anything that the RAG group wants to explore, from all the four days. This is an opportune moment for members to explore any experience, from any stage of the conference; to gain a further understanding, and make sense of organisational issues.

It's important that the consultant is able to provide containment for the group, especially on day two—the large study group; and day three—the inter-group event. Coming directly into the RAG from these experiences, there may be raw feelings that are brought into this group, which need to be regarded as further learning. It is important here that the consultant should stay in the role of RAG consultant and not revert to the here-and- now role. This will be an important factor in regard to containment.

Review will possibly take up half of the one and a half hours of the session. Having reviewed the most significant group as a whole dynamics on each day, when the time seems right to do so the consultant will start to move the group to an exploration of application to work situations, by asking if anyone could helpfully relate their understanding to similar experiences from their work organisations.

Application as experienced in the conference main events of each day

The consultant will open this process by asking: "What do you recall as the most significant role etc., in today's SSG event? And describe what this part of the task is about." Here, again, the essential focus is on the group-as-a-whole dynamics, rather than individual learning.

As was described above, on occasion the latter may also occur. Where this learning occurs, so be it, although not the essential aim, it should not be disregarded.

The skill of the consultant, in regard to application, is to help the members to explore the most significant group-as-a-whole experiences, in depth. Thus, it's not sufficient to simply accept that a member was mobilised into a flight leader role. It's important that the consultant seeks to get the members to explore why the member was mobilised, in a way that he might have interpreted in the here and now, including a "because clause". It's about going deeper, to beneath the surface: Why did the group mobilise the individual? If it was because of anxiety, what was causing the anxiety? Perhaps even asking the group: Why this particular member?

The process the consultant takes will be to address his questions to the whole group and invite any member of the RAG group to share their experiences of group-as-a-whole dynamics occurring in the workplace that are similar to that experienced in the main events of the day. Sharing this, and exploring this in public, will create and add to the depth of learning, particularly by those members in the same organisation, or the same work groups.

They may also share their experiences about what's been happening in the main event groups that day. These may or may not connect directly to back home experiences. The following are some examples of members applying their learning about group-as-a-whole dynamics to their organisations:

> Members of one RAG group described how they had been grappling with conflict in relation to an aggressive member. They were unsure whether they had been mobilising a fight leader, or, was the aggression the valency of this member, or both? The real issue was the need for understanding at a deeper level.
>
> Members of a second RAG group responded by describing how their group had "spent the day being very nice to each other", and avoiding any kind of conflict. Exploration helped members to see that each group was "doing something for the other" and for the whole system in managing, for example, an anxiety in relation to the primary task, which in this instance was learning.

An RAG group member who had been consulting to a school over a long period of time described how the headteacher was idealised by half the staff and demonised by the other half. And in spite of changes among all staff, including the head, this dynamic persisted. From his conference experiences, he learnt that he needed to change his focus and understand this dynamic in relation to the primary task. In other words, he needed to understand things at a deeper level.

Another member of an RAG group spoke of rivalry which was both uncomfortable and crippling to the work of her organisation but that she was beginning to see her part in it. This is a further example of where a member has learnt that they were now able to see things at a deeper level.

In all of these situations, the learning experience has enabled them, through application of the group-as-a-whole learning to understand their own roles and the deeper level of understanding that they have experienced in the various conference groups, to have a different perspective from that which they previously held; learning to apply conference learning to their experiences is an important outcome.

Post-conference organisational applications of conference learning

We will now apply this learning to our own experiences in organisations and other group experiences. These will all be examples arising from the dynamics described and explored in Chapters 1 to 5, confirming that whatever happens in conferences also happens in other personal and organisational groups, of different sizes.

In all organisations, there will exist a number of regular group meetings, for example, board meetings, management meetings, and project meetings. All these meetings will be structured and will have an agenda. Taking a normal example, several items on the agenda may be for information and will not require discussion. These items will be "nodded through" with little, if any, confusion. Other items may require discussion but the members present will be able to contribute in a conscious and collaborative manner to the agenda task, acting as a work group.

However, what may perhaps be the most important item on the agenda is that regarding resources—human or financial—which is experienced as a difficult task. In regard to this task, all members of the group are representing a team or group which is part of the organisation. The individual members at this meeting are going to be facing the expectancy of their team or group as to the determination of this task. Thus, any decision made in the meeting is likely to be criticised by team members.

A result may be that a great deal of anxiety is generated in the group as a whole. The group now mobilises a flight leader who leads the group in an avoidance of the task. If the chair of the meeting has been to a group relations conference and learned about basic assumption behaviour, he will recognise what's happening and encourage the group to return to their difficult task. However, if the chair is not aware of basic assumption behaviour, he will also become part of the basic assumption behaviour, whereby the task will be avoided. So, this highly important item on the agenda will not be determined. The avoidance may continue to the time boundary; at this point the chair may become concerned, whereby the other members of the group may suggest the chair make the decisions on their behalf.

Faced with little alternative, the chair agrees and takes it on him- or herself to make the decisions and let them all know what has been decided. Unfortunately, not having been consulted, when told of the decisions, the members disagree and demand that their views be heard, especially those with negative resource decisions. A likely outcome is the decision to confirm a further meeting, for this item only. Now the meeting will take place in anything but a conscious and collaborative manner. It will be a conflictual meeting where decisions are likely to be made without true agreement; most likely, with reluctance at the decisions made. Given the difficult task, there is likely to be anxiety. If the chair (or members) understand basic assumption behaviour there is a good chance that the group can remain a work group, working at this difficult task in a conscious and collaborative way. It is fair to say that learning from attendance at a group relations conference will give managers and leaders a competitive advantage in taking up their roles.

In a formal group such as a regular management team meetings there are always likely to be situations where conflicting ideas and feelings exist, and these are bound to surface in the meeting with every possibility that the members will suffer ensuing pain and anxiety. In these sorts of situations, the group is likely to regress from functioning as a work group to basic assumption functioning. Where the dominant basic assumption is dependency, a leader will be mobilised to take on the role of protector. This may be the formal leader or one of the other members of the group. A feature of this type of behaviour is that the members will unconsciously perceive who is a ready and suitable vehicle to provide this sort of leadership.

There is no actual demand for the individual to become leader, but rather there is an involuntary and instantaneous consideration of the leader taking on the role. When the basic assumption of dependency is active, the unconscious phantasy is that the group has come together in order to find security and protection from one individual alone, a dependency leader mobilised by the group. This individual is felt to be omniscient, possessing all the wisdom and solutions, while the other group members behave as if they know nothing and are devoid of resources and capacities. Very often, the member mobilised also accepts this position in the group and is drawn into enacting his part in this basic assumption, making all the decisions for the group and generally doing all the thinking. One can see immediately why it might be common for groups struggling to understand the task may fall into a basic assumption of dependency and to find a member who, they insist, is all-powerful, wise, and loving. Though the group strives to defend itself against inevitable disappointment by holding tenaciously to its conviction, invariably the leader disappoints and the group turns to mobilise a new leader, destined to suffer the same fate.

Bion's view was that valencies are part of the biological or physiological aspect of our psyche, part of human heritage. It was their very existence, he thought, that enabled the individual to become part of a group. Individual members of the group tend to be drawn into familiar roles through their own personal valencies. Some may have strong valencies to be the leader. It is not unusual for these individuals to be seen as work-group leaders: as successful task achievers. However, these individuals may frequently be mobilised by the group as a dependency leader, one who will make all the decisions, and push the group into completing the task. This gives the impression of it being a work group, but it is far from that. The group is not collaborating, it is simply "going along with" the leader and agreeing with his proposals for completing the task. This may be good or bad. However, it is only the work of one brain, whereas it could be the collaborative thinking and experience of (say) twelve people. In addition, through a participative (group-as-a-whole), conscious and collaborative process, all will own and be committed to decisions made.

Defensive structures based on basic assumption modes may become fixed in organisations in a way that can be described as social systems. For example, a work group may divide internally in response to difficult or risky conditions. This division then becomes a social defence: a system of relationships that helps people control and contain feelings of anxiety when facing their difficult work. As an example, a sales team may constantly be rejected in its attempts to make sales, this being in the nature of the role. The resulting feelings of incompetence are unbearable and too painful to live with. Consequently, the sales team unconsciously seeks out an individual or group that it can split off and project these feelings into. Frequently, this is an administrative or finance team which is then regarded as incompetent. The sales team can locate all incompetence on the admin or finance team and view itself as highly competent and able as practitioners. This collusive process which arises out of the extreme anxiety experienced by the sales force enables the organisation to compete by allowing the salespeople to conduct their task without fear of failure. But the price to pay is that the part of the organisation projected into will become incompetent.

Faced with extreme anxiety, a department or team may develop ways of avoiding the painful thoughts and feelings that become unbearable. An example concerned a health service organisation in which the members of the organisation, particularly those at admission and ward levels, were experiencing considerable stress and anxiety as a result of an attempt to treat an infinite number of patients with finite resources. The members of the organisation employed at the interface of the organisation and the environment who had to cope with what was sometimes an impossible task experienced feeling estrangement and abandonment which led to anger and hatred. Over a period of time, these feelings were split off and projected into the director of administration who then became an unloved, angry, and hated figure who was the repository of all badness in the organisation. As such, he was denigrated by the members of the organisation and experienced as a really nasty character who could be blamed for all painful experiences.

At the same time, the chief executive became the subject of all positive projections and was idealised by the members of the organisation. In this way, by locating all painful experiences in the director of administration, members of the organisation found a vehicle for their own unacceptable feelings. By idealising the chief executive, they created a phantasy that this wonderful person would ensure that they were safe and that no matter what happened, everything would be fine. This, of course, required the unconscious collusion of all members of the organisation, including the director of administration and the chief executive. The development of the social structure which was used as a defence against the anxiety of trying to perform an impossible task served to remove from awareness the unbearable thoughts and feelings evoked. However, what it did not do was to deal with the reality of the impossible task. A result was that patients were left waiting on trolleys, and a further result was that extreme stress and regular sickness was experienced by staff involved at the interface.

In the above example, the social structure as unconsciously developed was given objective existence in the social structure and culture of the organisation. As such, it was perpetuated and treated as an aspect of reality, as if the director of administration really was bad and the chief executive really was good. At one level, we might say that the effect of the defence system is to enable the members of the organisation in the continuance of the organisational tasks. However, at another level, it will be appreciated that it achieves nothing in regard to the original problem that was the source of the anxiety. Thus, while the social system is regarded as real and is an enduring feature of the social structure, it should not be forgotten that it is only in existence as a means of institutionalising primitive psychic defence mechanisms as an avoidance of anxiety.

A further health service example provides us with a serious warning of the potentially grave consequences of this sort of behaviour; and the need to go beyond a face-value view of perceived problems. At a group level, nurses on a ward may find the work so difficult and anxiety-provoking that they suffer from low self-esteem and experience thoughts of extreme incompetence and failure. For a group that needs to remain confident in the face of extreme pain and anxiety, these are unbearable thoughts and feelings. The danger is that they split these feelings off and locate them in another individual or group. In many wards, a convenient location for these split-off feelings are the cleaning staff who may be regarded as different because they are contracted in and are not part of the clinical staff. Should the nurses project into the cleaners these feelings of incompetence, they will be left feeling competent again. However, if the cleaners take in the projections and act upon them, they will be left feeling incompetent. A serious result may be that they perform as if they were incompetent, with a resulting poor standard of cleaning and a huge risk of infection by the "super bug" formally known as MRSA.

Unfortunately for task performance, members of organisations and institutions are likely to seek satisfaction of personal needs that are anti-task. Such social defences are likely to be anti-task as they relate in an unrealistic way. Very often, they need to mitigate the stresses and strains of the task itself and of confrontation with the human material on which the task is focused. In other words, members try to establish a social system that also acts as a defence against anxiety, both personal anxiety and that evoked by institutional membership. An example might concern a social service function such as an old people's home. Doubtless, the care of the aged and infirm is a difficult task, especially as many patients will suffer from a decreasing mental capacity and, in the worst cases, senile dementia. Faced with feelings of frustration and helplessness arising from the situation, members of the organisation will in most cases deal with this in an understanding manner, treating it as a reality situation and finding ways of owning their feelings. However, there have been occasions when members of such organisations have developed an unconscious phantasy that patients are what might be described as non-humans and have been denied the usual feelings associated with human beings. In this way, the members of the organisation blot out any feelings they may have had regarding their patients. A result is that they are no longer working to achieve the organisational task but are working towards a non-caring task that is in fact an anti-task.

This sort of anti-task social structure will appear in all aspects of the institution both formal and informal, in attitudes and interpersonal relations, in customs and conventions, and also, very significantly, in the actual formal social structure of the organisation and its management system. It is also important to appreciate that this is a collusive activity—a total group activity—whereby the individual, group, or subgroup is mobilised by the group as a whole to do something on behalf of the group and not as individuals: they are representing the group. In effect, this becomes the way things are done around here. Or in other words, it becomes part of the organisational culture.

An example of a group scapegoating a subgroup may be the sort of situation where a senior management team cannot deal with the painful thoughts and feelings associated with a failure to achieve the financial goals of the organisation. Faced with the possibility of having to make extremely unpopular decisions such as layoffs or even closure, they deal with this by splitting off the feelings of failure and locating them in a subgroup such as the sales force who they blame for all failings. This group, being one which is constantly living with fears of, and actual experiences of, failure, is a ready vehicle for these projections. This then becomes a feature of the organisation whereby the sales force is treated in reality as having been the cause of the organisation's problems.

External influences can bring great pressure on management who sometimes need to devise responses merely to survive. For example, during recent years, many organisations have been forced by fierce global competition to seek to remain competitive by cutting costs. There has followed a huge restructuring of organisations which has frequently resulted in mass redundancies which in turn affects the job security of those who remain. It has also taken out many management grades by way of introduction of flatter structures, thus removing opportunities for promotion. At a social subsystem level, this doubtless seemed a rational response to the perceived problems. However, at a psychological subsystem level, this response has been viewed unfavourably as the original structure and reward system were perceived by employees as the minimum obligations that they were owed by the organisation for their loyalty, conformity, and effort.

The consequences are predictable: employees are angry at the unilateral breaking of the psychological contract, and at the same time insecure, having lost trust in the organisation. And their feelings of inequity are increased by the disproportionate benefits enjoyed by top managers, who are perceived as fat cats. Moreover, many feel helpless in the absence of unions or other labour-market power to help them affect the situation. Overall, they have lost their previous feelings of commitment. But such issues of motivation and morale are vital since lean organisations need effort and commitment to get work done and a willingness to take risks in pursuit of innovation. Here, again, we have a seemingly rational approach to problem-solving that has not taken into consideration the beneath-the-surface dynamics. In the circumstances, it would not be surprising if an anti-task approach were taken by the members of the organisation.

Let's assume that one group, the senior management group, are concerned about racism in their organisation and realise that they may be as culpable, if not more culpable, than others. They deal with their unbearable thoughts and feelings by splitting them off and locating them in the lower levels of the organisation. The senior management team then, therefore, alter their uncomfortable experience by imagining that part of it is an attribute of something or someone else, rather than of themselves. Those at the lower levels of the organisation receive these denied and rejected feelings via projective identification and are subtly pressured into exhibiting racist behaviour.

In many organisations, what may be known as the rebellion leader will be regarded as a trouble-maker, the one who always goes to management with complaints and sometimes with threats of action if so and so is not done or perhaps undone. Seen in the context of the group as a whole this is every bit as much a social structure as the other situations referred to in previous examples. Whenever the members of the organisation are experiencing feelings of estrangement, a sense of not being alright, of not being nurtured, or put another way, a feeling that the organisational holding environment is not good enough, they may mobilise the rebellion leader who is induced to act on their behalf.

The rebellion leader is mobilised to carry and make the painful feelings known to management who are seen as being responsible for this painful situation and have the power to act to put it right. By mobilising the individual to act on their behalf, the other members of the group or organisation can remain safe from the prospect of driving away their managers who they need for their psychological and social safety and nurture as if they were mother. I should add that in most organisations my experience has been that the rebellion leader is frequently regarded and treated as a rather stupid person who is a nuisance. I take the view that if management wish to be aware of the feelings of the staff, they should listen very carefully to what this individual has to say because he is likely to be the only one who is truly expressing the feelings of the members of the organisation.

Change is inevitably, to some extent, an excursion into the unknown. It implies a commitment to future events that are not entirely predictable and to their consequences, and inevitably provokes doubt and anxiety. Any significant change within a social system implies changes in existing social relationships and in social structure. It follows that any significant social change implies a change in the operation of the social system as a defence against anxiety. While this change is proceeding—that is, while social defences are being restructured—anxiety is likely to be more open and intense. It has been stressed that resistance to social change can be better understood if it is seen as the resistance of groups of people unconsciously clinging to existing institutions because changes threaten existing social defences against deep and intense anxieties.

Every organisation has a task to sell a product or provide a service, a task the organisation has been formed to perform: what has been referred to as the "primary task". The major responsibility for the performance of that primary task are the operational groups or teams who are employed to sell the products or supply the services. They, therefore, bear the full, immediate, and concentrated impact of stress arising from the organisational task. By the nature of the task of the organisation or part of the organisation, there are many situations that develop in organisations where employees are flooded with intense and unmanageable anxiety. All sorts of situations can lead to high levels of distress, tension, and anxiety.

Where the organisation has failed to contain the high levels of anxiety and stress experienced by employees engaged in operational work, there may be a high level of tension, distress, and anxiety; as such, it becomes difficult to tolerate so much anxiety. The relief of the anxiety is an important task in providing containment that will enable them to engage in their task. It is important for managers and leaders to understand the nature of the anxiety and the reasons for its intensity.

The containing function is about noticing, receiving, and digesting primitive emotions, raw affect, incoherent states of mind in the team, damaging interactions, etc. The function should be located in management. Once digested, management takes decisions about what and how to feed back and what course of action to take and encourage.

Management needs to understand that these disturbances are necessary in periods of change. Their absence signals splitting and unhealthy, rigid denial caused by overwhelming anxiety, which the team members perceive management as too weak to handle—so they stop projecting, challenging, rebelling. A robust and healthy system will manage regression in the team and obtain much useful information from it—and must not deny or diminish it, otherwise it will be seen as fragile.

This requires a quality of leadership employing soft skills. Among these are: improved workplace communication, empathy, adaptability, collaboration, leadership and even culture-fit, problem-solving, positive attitude, emotional intelligence, and curiosity. The essential requirement regarding the way these matters can be communicated to staff and others is through the continual and consistent emotional content of the message as conveyed by managers and leaders. In other words, it is a message based on belief and emotional commitment that others perceive and identify with.

The behaviour observed in groups is not a product of groups as such but of the fact that the human being is a group animal. We carry our groupishness with us all the time. Physical assembly of people into a group simply makes "political" characteristics of human beings more easily demonstrable. However, physical assembly is not a prerequisite for the existence of a group. Take, for example, a group of personnel managers who were located in disparate parts of a large organisation. They seldom, if ever came together physically but they were still very much a group in the mind for those concerned. A family may no longer be part of the same physical home or even be in the same town or same country, but they will still regard themselves as a family group regardless of how often they may be together physically. Both the family and the personnel managers are not only part of a group in the mind but are very much related to each other in a mutually influential way.

An example might be the way a group of women might represent an unconscious dynamic in a group concerning a perceived or actual gender conflict within the group. At the surface level, in terms of what was being discussed in the group, there might be little if any indication of the unconscious processes that were occurring. But at a beneath-the-surface level, the unconscious formation and clustering of the women may be seen as a response to the underlying dynamics. By physically and psychologically coming together, they may be defending against an unconsciously perceived attack by the men in the group. At some point in the process, this unconscious activity may be triggered into conscious activity. Here we can see how the sum of the group as a whole is different from the individual group members.

Plenary discussion groups

Returning to our conferences, the plenary discussions are an opportunity to make further sense of the experience in discussion with the consultants, where necessary referring to theoretical concepts to assist the learning process.

A consultant will be delegated to mark the time boundaries, to inform the member of the task, or remind them of the task on later days. They will also encourage the members to take the opportunity for deeper learning: that there is an opportunity to ask questions or raise issues for discussion by all, members and consultants.

Following immediately after the RAG event, this session is a further opportunity to discuss application. This again is not a here-and-now event, but in general terms a further there-and-then event. Here consultants are willing to directly answer questions posed by members. However, the practice of consultants is still to encourage members to struggle for their own understanding. It is usual, then, that the question will first be posed by the consultants, to the members, asking if any other members are able to answer the question and, in some circumstances, to ask the questioner what they might think should be the answer. It may then be possible to suggest an experience from a session that will encourage a response to the question. It is only when there has been no helpful answers forthcoming that the consultants will supply an answer.

The more familiar behaviour by the consultants may prove to be a trigger for questions relating to the members' working experiences.

Being a non-residential conference, one of the aims of this event is to provide an experience similar to the usual teaching events which members are familiar with, and to return to their homes in a relatively contained manner.

Provision of papers each day

At the end of the discussion group, the papers relating to the main theme of the day will be distributed to the members. These papers will provide more theoretical understanding, which members can read at their leisure. If supplied in advance of the conference, these papers would have made little sense. However, having had the experience in the groups, they will recognise what has been happening to themselves and others, and will be able to assimilate experiences with theoretical understanding. This may result in a greater and deeper understanding that this is not just something that has happened in the conference, but that these behaviours are part of our personal and work lives. It opens their eyes to what is happening in the organisations they are working in.

The role of the administrator

Finally, a discussion of the important role of administrator. This person is the link and boundary keeper between the conference members and the outside world.

The role of the conference administrator is to provide administrative support to the conference director, staff, and members throughout the end-to-end group relations conference process.

The administrator is generally the first representative of the conference staff that the members meet on their arrival, welcoming them, and providing initial information. The aim is to create a safe and welcoming space from the start of the event. A pre-conference meeting with the director will ensure that the administrator is conversant with the specific venue and fully prepared to take up their role at the conference.

The role of the administrator is important in liaising with the conference venue and associated staff, to stress the importance of conference rooms being ready and refreshments available on time. The administrator will also stress the importance that rooms when in session are viewed as sacrosanct, and as such, not to be entered by anyone. In this way, the administrator ensures that the importance of the external boundaries of time and territory is clearly understood. Maintaining these external conference boundaries is one of the administrator's primary objectives. Situating the administrator in a physical position where they are able to monitor the external conference boundary, and protect this from threat, is ideal, although not always possible.

The administrator is included in all staff meetings from the pre-conference meeting onwards, to include all staff meetings throughout the conference. They will be asked to share information regarding the behaviour of the members, and news of any absentees. Their information regarding the members' relationships with the administrator and the way they behave towards them is vital information for the consulting staff to understand what is happening in the conference. Where, for example, frustration of members is projected towards the administrator, this and other relevant observations about the behaviour of the group during breaks is important knowledge in regard to the conference dynamics.

In a world where digital appliances are used extensively, during the conference members will be required to ensure that all devices are switched off during working sessions, to avoid disturbance to the learning process. Here, the administrator plays an important role in being available to take calls for members from outside the conference, locating members as soon as a working session ends, so that the member can return the call.

The administrator will not disturb groups even though callers may insist that it's urgent, but will tell the caller what time the member will be available to return the call.

A further vital role of the administrator is to identify members who may be intending to leave the conference, and inform them that they should not leave until they have been seen by the director or deputy director. At the next break, or other opportunity, the administrator will inform the director who will then meet with the member to establish why they were intending to leave. It may be something like a family emergency, in which case it may be decided that they leave immediately, but they may agree that they will return the next morning, if possible.

The vital task is that concerning a member who is not feeling well, having perhaps been projected into by the group. When that is the case, we don't want this member to leave without the group taking back their projections. What we want to avoid is a member returning home feeling overwhelmed and taking this into the family environment.

The following are two examples of how this can be important:

The first example concerns a woman projected into in a large-group situation, who, unbeknown to the administrator, left the conference and went home feeling unwell. Fortunately, another member informed the administrator who then contacted the director. It was then decided that the administrator would telephone the member and explain that the director wanted to talk with her. After the woman described what was happening to her, the director persuaded her to return, so that the group could take back their projections: this the woman did, and before the start of the next session (the discussion group), explained to all what had happened and asked them to take back their projections: this the group did. The woman very quickly recovered and took a full part in the session: a good conclusion.

In the next example, a woman with a very strong valency for taking a leadership role was found crying by the administrator. She called the director to see her. When asked why she was crying, she explained that the group was frequently mobilising her and using her to provide dependency leadership to the group, but would then reject her; this, of course, being the fate of all basic assumption leaders. He then ascertained that this is what frequently happens to her in her normal work role. Having heard the woman's story and experienced her pain and suffering, he suggested that she might avoid being mobilised by taking up an observer role for a session or more, until she felt able to rejoin the group. This she did, and successfully rejoined the group without being mobilised. This was also a very powerful learning through application.

This is one of those occasions where it might be considered that the director had gone out of role by taking a training role. However, it needs to be borne in mind that this was a totally conscious action by the director, working to the philosophy that "everything we do should be done for the benefit of the learning of the members".

To conclude, I hope that these chapters will also be seen as having been done for the benefit of the learning of you the reader.

References

Bion, W. R. (1952). Group dynamics: a re-view. *International Journal of Psychoanalysis*, *33*: 235–247.

Bion, W. R. (1961). *Experiences in Groups and Other Papers*. London: Tavistock.

Bion, W. R. (1992). *Cogitations*, F. Bion (Ed.). London: Karnac.

Freud, S. (1912e). Recommendations to physicians practising psycho-analysis. *S. E.*, *12*: 109–120. London: Hogarth.

Freud, S. (1915e). The unconscious. *S. E.*, *14*: 159–215. London: Hogarth.

Jaques, E. (1955). Social systems as a defence against persecutory and depressive anxiety: A contribution to the psychoanalytic study of social processes. In: M. Klein., P. Heimann., & R. E. Money-Kyrle (Eds.), *New Directions in Psychoanalysis: The Significance of Infant Conflict in the Pattern of Adult Behaviour* (pp. 478–498). London: Routledge.

Klein, M. (1940). Mourning and its relation to manic-depressive states. *International Journal of Psychoanalysis*, *21*: 125–153.

Klein, M. (1959). Our adult world and its roots in infancy. In: *Envy and Gratitude and Other Works*. London: Virago.

Le Bon, G. (1895). *Psychologie des Foules* [*The Crowd: A Study of the Popular Mind*]. New York: The Macmillan Company, 1897.

Lewin, K. (1951). *Field Theory in Social Science: Selected Theoretical Papers*, D. Cartwright (Ed.). New York: Harper & Row.

Menzies Lyth, I. E. P. (1960). A case-study in the functioning of social systems as a defence against anxiety: A report on a study of the nursing service of a general hospital. *Human Relations, 13*(2): 95–121.

Miller, E. J. (1989). The "Leicester" model: Experiential study of group and organizational processes. Tavistock Institute of Human Relations. Occasional Paper (10). London: Tavistock.

Miller, E. J., & Rice, A. K. (1967). *Systems of Organization: The Control of Task and Sentient Boundaries*. London: Tavistock.

Rice, A. K. (1965). *Learning for Leadership: Interpersonal and Intergroup Relations*. London: Tavistock.

Turquet, P. M. (1974). Leadership: The individual and the group. In: A. D. Colman & M. H. Geller (Eds.), (1985), *Group Relations Reader, 2*(2): 71–87.

Turquet, P. M. (1975). Threats to identity in the large group. In: L. Kreeger (Ed.), *The Large Group*. London: Karnac, 1994.

von Bertalanffy, L. (1950). The theory of open systems in physics and biology. *Science, 111*(2872): 23–29.

Index